COMPASSION

ALSO BY OSHO

COMPASSION

The Ultimate Flowering of Love

OSHO

·

Insights for a
New Way of Living

St. Martin's Griffin ✕ New York

DVD: OSHO TALK from the series *From Misery to Enlightenment*, #13, copyright © 1985, 2006 Osho International Foundation

Permission to reprint "The Thief Who Became a Disciple" from *Zen Flesh, Zen Bones*, compiled by Paul Reps, granted by Tuttle Publishing.

www.stmartins.com

www.osho.com

The material in this book is selected from various discourses by Osho given to a live audience over a period of more than thirty years. All of the Osho discourses have been published in full as books, and are also available as original audio recordings. Audio recordings and the complete text archive can be found via the online OSHO Library at www.osho.com.

OSHO is a registered trademark of Osho International Foundation, used with permission.

Library of Congress Cataloging-in-Publication Data

Osho, 1931–1990.
    Compassion : the ultimate flowering of love / Osho.
      p. cm.—(Insights for a new way of living)
    ISBN-13: 978-0-312-36568-4
    ISBN-10: 0-312-36568-3
    1. Spiritual life. 2. Compassion—Religious aspects. 3. Love—Religious aspects. I. Title.

BP605.R34C66 2007
299'.93—dc22

2006051158

First Edition: February 2007

10 9 8 7 6 5 4 3 2 1

Compassion is possible only with understanding and awareness. Not only do you understand and respect the other person, but you have come to your deepest core of being. Seeing your own deepest core, you have become capable of seeing the deepest core in the other also. Now the other does not exist as a body or a mind; the other exists as a soul. And souls are not separate; when two souls meet, they are one. Compassion is the highest form of love.

Contents

Preface

༄

We know what passion is; hence it is not very difficult to understand what compassion might be. Passion means a state of biological fever—it is hot, you are almost possessed by biological, unconscious energies. You are no longer your own master, you are just a slave.

Compassion means you have transcended biology, you have transcended physiology. You are no longer a slave, you have become a master. Now you function consciously. You are not driven, pulled and pushed by unconscious forces; you can decide what you want to do with your energies. You are totally free. Then the same energy that becomes passion is transformed into compassion.

Passion is lust, compassion is love. Passion is desire, compassion is desirelessness. Passion is greed, compassion is sharing. Passion wants to use the other as a means, compassion respects the other as an end unto himself or herself. Passion keeps you tethered to the earth, to the mud, and you never become a lotus. Compassion makes you a lotus. You start rising above the muddy world of desires, greed, anger. Compassion is a transformation of your energies.

Ordinarily you are scattered, fragmentary. Some energy is being absorbed by your anger, some energy is being absorbed by your greed, some energy is being absorbed by your lust, and so on and so forth. And there are so many desires surrounding you that you are left without any energy; you are left hollow, empty.

And remember what William Blake says—there is great insight in it—he says, "Energy is delight." But you don't have any energy left; all your energy keeps on going down the drain. When all these energies are no longer being wasted they start filling your inner lake, your inner being. You become full. A great delight arises in you. When you start overflowing, you have become a buddha and you have come upon an inexhaustible source.

And when you are a buddha, only then will you experience what compassion is. It is cool love—not cold, mind you—cool love. It is a sharing of your joy with the whole of existence. You become a blessing to yourself and a blessing to the whole existence. That is compassion. Passion is a curse, compassion is a blessing.

COMPASSION, ENERGY, AND DESIRE

~∂~

Buddha lived for forty years after he became enlightened. After all his desires were finished, the ego disappeared, he lived for forty years more. Many times it was asked, "Why are you still in the body?" When the business is finished you should disappear. It looks illogical: Why should Buddha exist in the body even for a moment longer? When there is no desire, how can the body continue?

There is something very deep to be understood. When desire disappears, the energy that was moving in desire remains; it cannot disappear. Desire is just a form of energy; that's why you can turn one desire into another. Anger can become sex, sex can become anger. Sex can become greed, so whenever you find a very greedy person he will be less sexual. If he is really perfectly greedy he will not be sexual at all, he will be a celibate—because the whole energy is moving into greed. And if you find a very sexual person you will always find that he is not greedy, because nothing is left over for greed. If you see a person who has suppressed his sexuality he will be angry; anger will be always ready to come to the surface. You can see in his eyes, in his face, that he is just angry; all the sex energy has become anger.

That's why your so-called monks and *sadhus* are always angry. The way they walk they show their anger; the way they look at you they show their anger. Their silence is just skin deep—touch them and they will become angry. Sex becomes anger. These are the forms; life is the energy.

What happens when all desires disappear? Energy cannot disappear, energy is indestructible. Ask the physicists; even they say that energy cannot be destroyed. A certain energy was existing in Gautam Buddha when he became enlightened. That energy had been moving in sex, anger, greed, in millions of ways. Then all those forms disappeared—so what became of that energy? Energy cannot go out of existence, and when desires are not there, it becomes formless but it still exists. Now what is the function of it? That energy becomes compassion.

You cannot be in compassion because you have no energy. All your energy is divided and spread into different forms—sometimes sex, sometimes anger, sometimes greed. Compassion is not a form. Only when all your desires disappear does your energy become compassion.

You cannot cultivate compassion. When you are desireless, compassion happens; your whole energy moves into compassion. And this movement is very different. Desire has a motivation in it, a goal; compassion is non-motivated; there is no goal to it. It is simply overflowing energy.

> Desire has a motivation in it, a goal, compassion is non-motivated, there is no goal to it. It is simply overflowing energy.

COMPASSION IS LOVE COME OF AGE

Gautam Buddha's emphasis on compassion was a new phenomenon as far as the mystics of old were concerned. Gautam Buddha creates an historical dividing line from the past. Before him, meditation was enough; nobody had emphasized compassion together with meditation. And the reason was that meditation brings enlightenment, your blossoming, your ultimate expression of being—what more do you need? As far as the individual is concerned, meditation is enough. Buddha's greatness consists in introducing compassion even before you start meditating. You should be more loving, more kind, more compassionate.

There is a hidden science behind it. Before you become enlightened, if you have a heart full of compassion there is a possibility that after meditation you will help others to achieve the same beauty, the same height, the same celebration as you have achieved. Gautam Buddha makes it possible for enlightenment to be infectious.

But if the person feels that he has come back home, why bother about anybody else? Buddha makes enlightenment for the first time unselfish; he makes it a social responsibility. It is a great change in perspective. But compassion should be learned before enlightenment happens. If it is not learned before, then after enlightenment there is nothing to learn. When one becomes so ecstatic in oneself, then even compassion seems to be preventing one's own joy, a kind of disturbance in one's ecstasy. That's why there have been hundreds of enlightened people, but very few masters.

To be enlightened does not mean necessarily that you will become a master. Becoming a master means you have tremendous compassion, and you feel ashamed to go alone into those beautiful spaces that enlightenment makes available. You want to help the people who are blind, in darkness, groping their way. It becomes a joy to help them, it is not a disturbance. In fact, it becomes a richer ecstasy when you see so many people flowering around you; you are not a solitary tree who has blossomed in a forest where no other tree is blossoming. When the whole forest blossoms with you, the joy grows a thousandfold; you have used your enlightenment to bring a revolution in the world.

Gautam Buddha is not only enlightened, but an enlightened revolutionary. His concern with the world, with people, is immense. He was teaching his disciples that when you meditate and you feel silence, serenity, a deep joy bubbling inside your being, don't hold onto it; give it to the whole world. And don't be worried, because the more you give it, the more you will become capable of getting it. The gesture of giving is of tremendous importance once you know that giving does not take anything from you; on the contrary, it multiplies your experiences. But one who has never been compassionate does not know the secret of giving, does not know the secret of sharing.

It happened that one of Buddha's disciples, a layman—he was not a sannyasin but he was very devoted to Gautam Buddha—said, "I will do it . . . but I want just to make one exception. I will give all my joy and all my meditation and all my inner treasures to the whole world— except my neighbor, because that fellow is really nasty."

Neighbors are always enemies. Gautam Buddha said to him, "Then forget about the world, you simply give to your neighbor."

The man was at a loss: "What are you saying?"

Buddha said, "If you can give to your neighbor, only then will you be freed from this antagonistic attitude towards the human being."

Compassion basically means accepting people's frailties, their weaknesses, not expecting them to behave like gods. That expectation is cruelty, because they will not be able to behave like gods and then they will fall in your estimation and will also fall in their own self-respect. You have dangerously crippled them, you have damaged their dignity.

One of the fundamentals of compassion is to dignify everybody, to make everybody aware that what has happened to you can happen to them; that nobody is a hopeless case, nobody is unworthy, that enlightenment is not something to be deserved, it is your very self-nature.

But these words should come from the enlightened person, only then can they create trust. If they come from unenlightened scholars, the words cannot create trust. The word, spoken by the enlightened man, starts breathing, starts having a heartbeat of its own. It becomes alive, it goes directly into your heart—it is <u>not intellectual gymnastics</u>. But with the scholar it is a different thing. He himself is not certain of what he is talking about, what he is writing about. He is in the same uncertainty as you are.

Gautam Buddha is one of the landmarks in the evolution of consciousness; his contribution is great, immeasurable. And in his contribution the idea of compassion is the most essential. But you have to remember that in being compassionate you don't become higher; otherwise you spoil the whole thing. It becomes an ego trip. Remember not to humiliate the other person by being compassionate; other-wise you are not being compassionate—behind the words you are enjoying their humiliation.

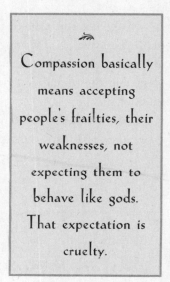

Compassion basically means accepting people's frailties, their weaknesses, not expecting them to behave like gods. That expectation is cruelty.

Compassion has to be understood, because it is love come of age. Ordinary love is very childish, it is a good game for teenagers. The faster you grow out of it the better, because your love is a blind biological force. It has nothing to do with your spiritual growth; that's why all love affairs turn in a strange way, become very bitter. That which was so alluring, so exciting, so challenging, that for which you could have died . . . now you could still die, but not for it, you could die to get rid of it!

Love is a blind force. The only successful lovers have been those who never succeeded in getting their beloveds. All the great stories of lovers . . . Laila and Majnu, Shiri and Farhad, Soni and Mahival, these are the three Eastern stories of great love, comparable to Romeo and Juliet. But all these great lovers could not get together. The society, the parents, everything became a barrier. And I think perhaps it was good. Once lovers get married, then there is no love story left.

Majnu was fortunate that he never got hold of Laila. What happens when two blind forces come together? Because both are blind and unconscious, the outcome cannot be a great harmony. The outcome can only be a battlefield of domination, of humiliation, all kinds of conflicts.

But when passion becomes alert and aware, the whole energy of love comes to a refinement; it becomes compassion. Love is always addressed to one person, and its deepest desire is to possess that person. The same is the case from the other side—and it creates hell for both people.

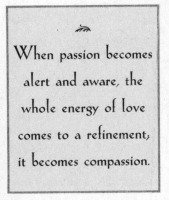

When passion becomes alert and aware, the whole energy of love comes to a refinement; it becomes compassion.

Compassion is not addressed to anybody. It is not a relationship, it is simply your very being. You enjoy being compassionate to the trees, to the birds, to the animals, to human beings, to everybody—unconditionally, not asking for anything in return. Compassion is freedom from blind biology.

Before you become enlightened, you should keep alert that your love energy is not repressed. That's what old religions have been doing: they teach you to condemn the biological expressions of your love. So you repress your love energy . . . and that is the energy that can be transformed into compassion!

With condemnation, there is no possibility of transformation. So your saints are absolutely without any compassion; in their eyes you will not see any compassion. They are absolutely dry bones, with no juice at all. To live with a saint for twenty-four hours is enough to experience what hell is like. Perhaps people are aware of this fact, so they touch the feet of the saint and run away immediately.

One of the great philosophers of our age, Bertrand Russell, has emphatically declared, "If there is hell and heaven, I want to go to hell." Why? Just to avoid the saints, because heaven will be full of all these dead, dull, dusty saints. And Bertrand Russell thinks, "I could not tolerate this company even for a minute. And to imagine spending eternity, forever, surrounded by these corpses who don't know any love, who don't know any friendship, who never go on holidays . . . !?"

A saint remains seven days a week a saint. It is not allowed to him that at least on one day, Sunday, he should enjoy being a human being. No, he remains stiff, and this stiffness goes on growing as time passes.

Bertrand Russell's choice to be in hell I appreciate very much, because I can understand what he means by it. He is saying that in hell you will find all the juicy people of the world—the poets, the painters, the rebellious spir-

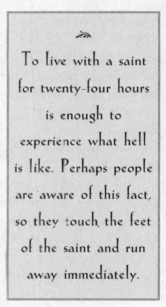

To live with a saint for twenty-four hours is enough to experience what hell is like. Perhaps people are aware of this fact, so they touch the feet of the saint and run away immediately.

its, the scientists, the creative people, the dancers, the actors, the singers, the musicians. Hell must be really a heaven, because heaven is nothing but a hell!

Things have gone so wrong, and the basic reason for their going wrong is that love energy has been repressed. Gautam Buddha's contribution is, "Don't repress your love energy. Refine it, and use meditation to refine it." So, side by side, as meditation grows it goes on refining your love energy and makes it compassion. Then, before your meditation reaches its highest climax and explodes into a beautiful experience of enlightenment, compassion will be very close. It will become possible for the enlightened person to let his energies flow—and now he has all the energies of the world—through the roots of compassion, to anyone who is ready to receive. Only this type of person becomes a master.

To become enlightened is simple, but to become a master is a very complex phenomenon, because it needs meditation plus compassion. Just meditation is easy, just compassion is easy; but both together, simultaneously growing, becomes a complex affair.

But the people who become enlightened and never share their experience because they don't feel any compassion don't help the evolution of consciousness on the earth. They don't raise the level of humanity. Only the masters have been able to raise consciousness. Whatever small consciousness you have, the whole credit goes to the few masters who managed to remain compassionate, even after their enlightenment.

It will be difficult for you to understand . . . but enlightenment is so absorbing that one tends to forget the whole world. One is so utterly satisfied that he does not have any space to think of all those millions who are also groping for the same experience, knowingly or unknowingly, rightly or wrongly. When compassion remains present, then it is impossible to forget those people. In fact, this is the moment when you have something to give, something to share. And sharing is such a joy. You have known through compassion, slowly, that the more you share the more you have. If you can share your enlightenment too, your enlightenment will have much more richness, much more aliveness, much more celebration, many more dimensions.

Enlightenment can be one-dimensional—that's what has happened to many people. It satisfies them, and they disappear into the universal source. But enlightenment can be multidimensional, it can bring so many flowers to the world. And you owe something to the world because you are sons and daughters of this earth.

I am reminded of Zarathustra's saying: "Never betray the earth. Even in your highest glory, don't forget the earth; it is your mother. And don't forget the people. They may have been hindrances, they may have been enemies to you. They may have tried in every way to destroy you; they may have already crucified you, stoned you to death, or poisoned you—but don't forget them. Whatever they have done, they have done in an unconscious state. If you cannot forgive them, who is going to forgive them? And your forgiving them is going to enrich you immeasurably."

Just watch that you don't give any support to anything that goes against compassion. Jealousy, competition, an effort to dominate—all that goes against compassion. And you will know immediately because your compassion will start wavering. The moment you feel your compassion is shaky, you must be doing something that is going against it. You can poison your compassion by stupid things which don't give you anything except anxiety, anguish, struggle, and a sheer wastage of a tremendously precious life.

A beautiful story for you:

> Paddy came home an hour earlier than usual and found his wife stark naked on the bed. When he asked why, she explained, "I am protesting because I don't have any nice clothes to wear."
>
> Paddy pulled open the closet door. "That's ridiculous," he said, "look in here. There is a yellow dress, a red dress, a print dress, a pantsuit . . . Hi, Bill!" And he goes on, "A green dress . . ."

This is compassion! It is compassion to his wife, it is compassion to Bill. No jealousy, no fight, just simply, "Hi, Bill! How are you?"

and he goes on. He never even inquires, "What are you doing in my closet?"

Compassion is very understanding. It is the finest understanding that is possible to man.

A man of compassion should not be disturbed by small things in life, which are happening every moment. Only then, in an indirect way, are you helping your compassionate energies to accumulate, to crystallize, to become stronger, and to go on rising with your meditation. So the day the blissful moment comes, when you are full of light, there will be at least one companion—compassion. And immediately a new style of life . . . because now you have so much that you can bless the whole world.

Although Gautam Buddha insisted constantly, finally he had to make a division, a categorization amongst his disciples. One category he calls *arhatas*; they are enlightened people, but without compassion. They have put their whole energy into meditation, but they have not listened to what Buddha has said about compassion. And the other he calls *bodhisattvas*; they have listened to his message of compassion. They are enlightened with compassion, so they are not in a hurry to go to the other shore; they want to linger on this shore, with all kinds of difficulties, to help people. Their boat has arrived, and perhaps the captain is saying, "Don't waste time, the call has come from the other shore which you have been seeking all your life." But they persuade the captain to wait a little, so that they can share their joy, their wisdom, their light, their love with all those people who are also searching the same. This will become a feeling of trust in them: "Yes, there is another shore, and when one is ripe, a boat comes to take you to the other shore. There is a shore of immortals, there is a shore where no misery exists, where life is simply a moment-to-moment song and a dance. But let me at least give these people a little taste before I leave the world."

And masters have tried in every possible way to cling to something so that they are not swept away to the other shore. According to Buddha, compassion is the best, because compassion is also a desire, in the final analysis. The idea to help somebody is also a desire, and as long as you keep the desire you cannot be taken to the other shore. It is a very thin thread that keeps you attached to the world. Everything is broken, all chains are broken—except a thin thread of love. But Buddha's emphasis is, keep hold of that thin thread as long as possible; as many people that can be helped, help them.

Your enlightenment should not have a selfish motive, it should not be just yours; you should make it shared as widely, to as many people, as possible. That's the only way to raise the consciousness on the earth—which has given you life, which has given you the chance to become enlightened.

This is the moment to pay back something, although you cannot pay back everything that life has given to you. But something—just two flowers—in gratitude.

MEDITATION THE FLOWER AND COMPASSION THE FRAGRANCE

Meditation is a flower and compassion is its fragrance.

Exactly like that it happens. The flower blooms and the fragrance spreads on the winds in all directions, to be carried to the very ends of earth. But the basic thing is the blooming of the flower.

Man is also carrying a potentiality for flowering within him. Until and unless the inner being of man flowers, the fragrance of compassion is not possible. Compassion cannot be practiced. It is not a discipline. You cannot manage it. It is beyond you. If you meditate, one day, suddenly, you become aware of a new phenomenon, absolutely strange—from your being, compassion is flowing towards the whole of existence. Undirected, unaddressed, it is moving to the very ends of existence.

Without meditation, energy remains passion; with meditation, the same energy becomes compassion. Passion and compassion are not two energies, they are one and the same energy. Once it passes through meditation it is transformed, transfigured; it becomes qualitatively different. Passion moves downwards, compassion moves upwards; passion moves through desire, compassion moves through desirelessness; passion is an occupation to forget the miseries in which you live, compassion is a celebration, it is a dance of attainment, of fulfillment . . . you are so fulfilled that you can share. Now there is nothing left; you have attained the destiny that you were carrying for millennia within you like an unflowered potentiality, just a bud. Now it has flowered and it is dancing. You have attained, you are fulfilled, there is no more to attain, nowhere to go, nothing to do.

> ༄
>
> Without meditation, energy remains passion, with meditation, the same energy becomes compassion. Passion and compassion are not two energies, they are one and the same.

Now what will happen to the energy? You start sharing. The same energy that was moving through the dark layers of passion, now moves with light rays upwards, uncontaminated by any desire, uncontaminated by any conditioning. It is uncorrupted by any motivation—hence I call it fragrance. The flower is limited but not the fragrance. The flower has limitations—it is rooted somewhere in bondage. But fragrance has no bondage. It simply moves, rides on the winds; it has no moorings in the earth.

Meditation is a flower. It has roots. It exists in you. Once compassion happens, it is not rooted; it simply moves and goes on moving. Buddha has disappeared but not his compassion. The flower will die sooner or later—it is part of the earth and the dust will return unto dust—but the fragrance that has been released will remain forever and forever. Buddha has gone, Jesus has gone, but not their fragrance.

Their compassion still continues and whoever is open to their compassion will immediately feel its impact, will be moved by it, will be taken on a new journey, on a new pilgrimage.

Compassion is not limited to the flower—it comes from the flower but it is not of the flower. It comes through the flower, the flower is just a passage. But it comes really from the beyond. It cannot come without the flower—the flower is a necessary stage—but it does not belong to the flower. Once the flower has bloomed, compassion is released.

This insistence, this emphasis, has to be deeply understood, because if you miss the point you can start practicing compassion but then it is not real fragrance. A practiced compassion is just the same passion with a new name. It is the same desire-contaminated, motivation-corrupted energy and it can become very dangerous to other people—because in the name of compassion you can destroy, in the name of compassion, you can create bondage. It is not compassion, and if you practice it you are being artificial, formal—in fact , a hypocrite.

The first thing to be remembered is that compassion cannot be practiced. It is this point where all the followers of all the great religious teachers have missed. Buddha attained compassion through meditation—now Buddhists go on practicing compassion. Jesus attained compassion through meditation—now Christians, the Christian missionaries, go on practicing love, compassion, service to humanity but their compassion has proved to be a very destructive force in the world. Their compassion has created only wars; their compassion has destroyed millions of people. They end up in deep imprisonments.

Compassion frees you, gives you freedom, but that compassion has to come only through meditation, there is no other way to it. Buddha has said that compassion is a by-product, a consequence. You cannot catch hold of the consequence directly, you have to move; you have to produce the cause, and the effect follows. So if you really want to understand what compassion is you have to understand what meditation is. Forget all about compassion; it comes of its own accord.

Try to understand what meditation is. Compassion can become a criterion as to whether the meditation was right or not. If the meditation has been right, compassion is bound to come—it is natural; it follows like a shadow. If the meditation has been wrong then compassion will not follow. So compassion can work as a criterion as to whether the meditation has been really right or not. And a meditation can be wrong. People have a wrong notion that all meditations are right. It is not so. Meditations can be wrong. For example, any meditation that leads you deep into concentration is wrong—it will not result in compassion. You will become more and more closed rather than becoming open. If you narrow down your consciousness, concentrate on something, and you exclude the rest of existence and become one-pointed, it will create more and more tension in you. Hence the word "attention." It means "at-tension." Concentration, the very sound of the word, gives you a feeling of tenseness.

Concentration has its uses but it is not meditation. In scientific work, in scientific research, in the science lab, you need concentration. You have to concentrate on one problem and exclude everything else—so much so that you almost become unmindful of the remaining world. Your world is only the problem you are concentrating upon. That's why scientists become absentminded. People

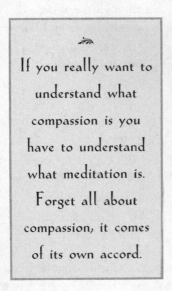

If you really want to understand what compassion is you have to understand what meditation is. Forget all about compassion, it comes of its own accord.

who concentrate too much always become absentminded because they don't know how to remain open to the whole world.

I was reading an anecdote:

"I have brought a frog," said the professor of zoology, beaming at his class, "fresh from the pond, in order that we might study its outer appearance and later dissect it."

He carefully unwrapped the package he carried, and inside was a neatly prepared ham sandwich. The good professor looked at it with astonishment.

"Odd!" he said, "I distinctly remember having eaten my lunch."

That goes on happening to scientists. They become one-pointed and their whole mind becomes narrow. Of course, a narrow mind has its use: It becomes more penetrating, it becomes like a sharp needle, it hits exactly the right point, but it misses the great life that surrounds it.

A buddha is not a man of concentration, he is a man of awareness. He has not been trying to narrow down his consciousness; on the contrary, he has been trying to drop all barriers so that he becomes totally available to existence. Watch . . . existence is simultaneous. I am speaking here and the traffic noise is simultaneous. The train, the birds, the wind blowing through the trees—in this moment the whole of existence converges. You listening to me, I speaking to you, and millions of things going on—it is tremendously rich.

Concentration makes you one-pointed at a very great cost: Ninety-nine percent of life is discarded. If you are solving a mathematical problem, you cannot listen to the birds—they will be a distraction. Children playing around, dogs barking in the street—they will be a distraction. Because of concentration, people have tried to escape from life—to go to the Himalayas, to go to a cave, to remain isolated so they can concentrate on God. But God is not an object.

God is this wholeness of existence, this moment; God is the totality. That's why science will never be able to know godliness. The very method of science is concentration and because of that method, science can never know the divine.

It can know more and more minute details. First the molecule was thought to be the smallest particle, then it was divided. Then an even tinier part, the atom, was known. Then the methods of concentration divided that also. Now there are electrons, protons, neutrons—sooner or later they are also going to be divided. Science goes on from the smaller to the smaller, and the bigger, the vast, is completely forgotten. The whole is completely forgotten for the part. Science can never know godliness because of concentration. So when people come to me and they say, "Osho, teach us concentration, we want to know the divine," I'm simply puzzled. They have not understood the basics of the search.

Science is one-pointed; the search is objective. Religiousness is simultaneity; the object is the whole, the total. To know the total, you will have to have a consciousness that is open on all sides—not confined, not standing in a window; otherwise the frame of the window will become the frame of existence. Just standing under the sun in the open sky—that is what meditation is. Meditation has no frame; it is not a window, it is not a door.

Meditation is not concentration, it is not attention—meditation is awareness.

So what to do? Repeating a mantra, doing transcendental meditation, is not going to help. Transcendental meditation has become very important in America because of the objective approach, because of the scientific mind. And it has been the only meditation on which scientific research can be done. It is concentration and not meditation, so it is comprehensible to the scientific mind. In the universities, in the laboratories, in psychological research work, much research has been done on TM because it is *not* meditation. It is concentration, a method of concentration; it falls under the same category as scientific concentration; there is a link between the two. But it has nothing to do with meditation. Meditation is so vast, so tremendously infinite, that no scientific research is possible. Only compassion will demonstrate whether the person has achieved it or not. Alpha waves won't be of much help, because they are still of the mind and meditation is not of the mind—it is something beyond.

So, let me tell you a few basic things. One, meditation is not concentration but relaxation—one simply relaxes into oneself. The more you relax, the more you feel yourself open, vulnerable. You are less rigid, you are more flexible—and suddenly existence starts penetrating you. You are no longer like a rock, you have openings. Relaxation means allowing yourself to fall into a state where you are not doing anything, because if you are doing something, tension will continue. It is a state of non-doing. You simply relax and you enjoy the feeling of relaxation. Relax into yourself, just close your eyes, and listen to all that is happening all around. No need to feel anything as distraction. The moment you feel it is a distraction, you are denying the divine. This moment it has come to you as a bird. Don't turn it away! The divine has knocked at your door as a bird. The next moment it has come as a dog barking, or as a child crying and weeping, or as a madman laughing. Don't deny it; don't reject it.

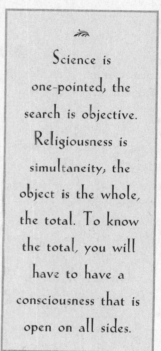

Science is one-pointed, the search is objective. Religiousness is simultaneity, the object is the whole, the total. To know the total, you will have to have a consciousness that is open on all sides.

Accept—because if you deny anything you will become tense. All denials create tension. Accept. If you want to relax, acceptance is the way. Accept whatever is happening all around; let it become an organic whole. It is—you may know it or you may not know it, but everything is interrelated. These birds, these trees, this sky, this sun, this earth, you, me—all are related. It is an organic unity. If the sun disappears, the trees will disappear; if the trees disappear, the birds will disappear; if the birds and trees disappear, you cannot be here, you will disappear. It is an ecology. Everything is deeply related with everything else. So don't deny anything, because the moment you deny, you are denying something in you. If you deny these singing birds then something in you is denied.

> If you want to relax, acceptance is the way. Accept whatever is happening all around, let it become an organic whole. It is—you may know it or you may not know it, but everything is interrelated.

If you deny, reject, if you feel distracted, if you feel angry, you are rejecting something within you. Just listen again to the birds without any feeling of distraction, anger, and suddenly you will see that the bird within you responds. Then those birds are not there as strangers, intruders—suddenly the whole existence becomes a family. It is, and I call a person religious who has come to understand that the whole existence is a family. He may not go to any church, he may not worship in any temple, he may not pray at any mosque or gurudwara—that doesn't matter, it is irrelevant. If you do, good, it is okay; if you don't that is even better. But one who has understood the organic unity of existence is constantly in the temple, is constantly facing the sacred and the divine.

But if you are doing some stupid mantra you will think the birds are stupid. If you are repeating some nonsense within you, or thinking some trivia—you may call it philosophy, religion—then the birds become distractions. Their sounds are simply divine. They don't say anything, they are simply bubbling with delight. Their song has no meaning except an overflowing of energy. They want to share with existence, with the trees, with the flowers, with you. They have nothing to say; they are just being there, themselves.

If you relax, you accept; acceptance of existence is the only way to relax. If small things disturb you then it is your attitude that is disturbing you. Sit silently; listen to all that is happening all around, and relax. Accept, relax—and suddenly you will feel immense energy arising in you. That energy will be felt first as a deepening of your breath. Ordinarily your breath is very shallow and sometimes if you try to take deep breaths, if you start doing yoga exercises with your breathing, start forcing something, you make an effort. That effort is not needed. You simply accept life, relax, and suddenly you will see that your breath is going deeper. Relax more and the breath goes deeper in you. It becomes slow, rhythmic, and you can almost enjoy it; it gives a certain delight. Then you will become aware that breath is the bridge between you and the whole.

Just watch. Don't do anything. And when I say watch, don't *try* to watch, otherwise you will become tense again and you will start concentrating on the breath. Simply relax, remain relaxed, loose, and look . . . because what else can you do? You are there, nothing to be done, everything accepted, nothing to be denied, rejected, no struggle, no fight, no conflict, breathing going deep—what can you do? You simply watch. Remember, simply watch. Don't make an effort to watch. This is what Buddha has called *vipassana*—the watching of the breath, awareness of the breath. Or *satipatthana*—remembering, being alert to the life energy that moves in breath. Don't try to take deep breaths, don't try to inhale or exhale, don't do anything. You simply relax and let the breathing be natural—going on its own, coming on its own—and many things will become available to you.

The first thing will be that breathing can be taken in two ways because it is a bridge. One part of it is joined with you, another part is joined with existence. So it can be understood in two ways. You can take it as a voluntary thing. If you want to inhale deeply, you can inhale deeply; if you want to exhale deeply, you can exhale deeply. You can do something about it. One part is joined with you. But if you don't do anything, then too it continues. No need for you to do anything and it continues. It is non-voluntary also.

The other part is joined with existence itself. You can think of it as if you are taking it in, you are breathing it, or you can think in just the opposite way—that it is breathing you. And the other way has to be understood because that will lead you into deep relaxation. It is not that you are breathing, but existence is breathing you. It is a change of gestalt, and it happens on its own. If you go on relaxing, accepting everything, relaxing into yourself, by and by, suddenly, you become aware that you are not taking these breaths—they are coming and going on their own. And so gracefully. With such dignity. With such rhythm. With such harmonious rhythm. Who is doing it? Existence is breathing you. It comes into you, goes out of you. Each moment it rejuvenates you, each moment it makes you alive again and again and again.

Suddenly you see breathing as a happening . . and this is how meditation should grow. And this you can do anywhere, in the marketplace also, because that noise is also divine. And if you listen silently, even in the marketplace you will see a certain harmony in the noise. It is no longer a distraction. You can see many things if you are silent—tremendous waves of energy moving all around. Once you accept, wherever you go you will feel it.

The bird is not important but you will feel something tremendously great, you will feel something holy, something luminous, something mysterious. A miracle is constantly happening all around you but you go on missing it.

Once meditation settles in you and you fall into rhythm with existence, compassion is a consequence. Suddenly you feel you are in love with the whole and the other is no longer the other—in the other also you live. And the tree is no longer just "that tree," somehow it is related to you. Everything becomes interrelated. You touch a leaf of grass and you have touched all the stars because everything is related. It cannot be otherwise. Existence is organic. It is one. It is a unity.

Because we are not aware we don't see what we go on doing to ourselves. One thing happens and something which you have never thought that it was related to starts happening.

Just the other night I was reading something about smell. The sensation, the capacity of smell, has almost disappeared from humanity. Animals are very sharp. A horse can smell for miles. A dog can smell more than a man. Just by the smell the dog knows that his master is coming, and after many years the dog will again recognize the smell that is his master's smell. Man has completely forgotten.

What has happened to people's sense of smell? What calamity has happened to it? There seems to be no reason why the sense of smell has been so suppressed. No culture anywhere has consciously suppressed it, but it has become suppressed. It has become suppressed because of sex. Now, the whole of humanity lives with sex deeply suppressed—and smell is connected with sex. Before making love, a dog will smell the partner and unless he smells a harmony deep down between the two bodies, he will not make love. Once the smell is fitting then he knows that now the bodies are in tune and they can fit and they can become a song—even for a moment, unity is possible.

Because sex has been suppressed all over the world, the sense of smell has become suppressed. The very word has become a little condemnatory. If I say to you, "Do you hear?" or "Do you see?" you don't feel offended. So if I say, "Do you smell?" one should not feel offended either, it is the same language. Smell is a capacity; just like seeing and hearing, smelling is a capacity. When I ask, "Do you smell?" one feels offended because one has completely forgotten that it is a capacity and not a condemnation.

There is a famous anecdote about an English thinker, Dr. Johnson. He was sitting in a stagecoach and a lady entered. She said to Dr. Johnson, "Sir, you smell!"

But he was a man of language, letters, a grammarian. He said, "No, madam. You smell. I stink!"

Smell is a capacity. "You smell. I stink." Linguistically he is right. That's how it should be if you follow grammar. But the very word has become condemnatory. What has happened to smell? Once you suppress sex, the sense of smell is suppressed. One sense is completely crippled—and if you cripple one sense then one part of the mind is crippled, too. If you have five senses, then your brain has five corresponding parts. One fifth of the brain is crippled and one never knows it. That means one fifth of life is crippled. The implications are tremendous. If you touch a small thing somewhere it reverberates all over.

Because of repressing sex, smell has been repressed, and because of repressing sex your breathing has become shallow—because if you breathe deep, your breathing massages the sex center inside. People come to me and say, "If we really breathe, we feel more sexual." If you make love to a partner your breathing will become very deep. If you keep your breathing shallow, you will not be able to achieve orgasm. The breathing hits hard, deep down in the sex center; from within it massages the sex center. Because sex has been repressed, and because breathing is repressed, people have become incapable of meditation. Now look at the whole thing—what nonsense we have done! Repressing sex, we have repressed breathing—and breathing is the only bridge between you and the whole.

Gurdjieff is right when he says that almost all religions have behaved in such a way that they seem to be against God. They talk about God but they seem to be basically against godliness. The way they have behaved is against it. Now that breathing is repressed, the bridge is broken. You can only breathe shallowly—you never go deep, and if you cannot go deep into yourself, you cannot go deep into existence.

Buddha makes breathing the very foundation. A deep, relaxed breathing, an awareness of it, gives you such tremendous silence, relaxation, by and by you simply merge, melt, disappear. You are no longer a separate island, you start vibrating with the whole. Then you are not a separate note but part of this whole symphony. Then compassion arises. Compassion arises only when you can see that everybody is related to you. Compassion arises only when you see that you are a member of everybody and everybody is a member of you. Nobody is separate. When the illusion of separation drops, compassion arises. Compassion is not a discipline.

In the human experience, the relationship between a mother and her child is the closest to compassion. People call it love but it should not be called love. It is more like compassion

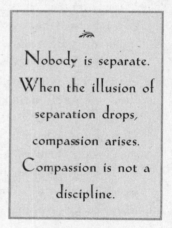

Nobody is separate. When the illusion of separation drops, compassion arises. Compassion is not a discipline.

than love, because it has no passion in it. A mother's love for the child is closest to compassion. Why? Because the mother has known the child in herself; the child was a member of her being. She has known the child as part of herself and even if the child is born and is growing, the mother goes on feeling a subtle rhythm with the child. If the child feels ill, a thousand miles away the mother will immediately feel it. She may not be aware of what has happened but she will become depressed; she may not be aware that her child is suffering but she will start suffering. She will create some rationalization about why she is suffering—her stomach is not okay, she has a headache, or something or other—but now, depth psychology says that the mother and the child always remain joined together with subtle energy waves, because they go on vibrating on the same wavelength.

Telepathy is easier between a mother and her child than between any other set of people. The same is the case with twins—between twins, telepathy is very easy. Many experiments on telepathy have been done in Soviet Russia—not of course for religious exploration but because they were trying to find out if telepathy could be used as a technique in war. They found that twins are very telepathic. If one twin has a cold, a thousand miles away the other also gets a cold. They vibrate on the same wavelength, they are affected by the same things. It is because they have both lived in the same womb as part of each other; they have existed in the mother's womb together.

A mother's feeling for the child is more like compassion because she feels the child is her own.

I was reading an anecdote:

During the preliminary inspection of a Boy Scout camp, the director found a large umbrella hidden in the bedroll of a tiny scout, obviously not one of the items of equipment listed. The director asked the lad to explain. The tenderfoot did so neatly by asking, "Sir, did you ever have a mother?"

Mother means compassion, mother means feeling for the other as one feels for oneself. When a person moves deeply in meditation and becomes enlightened, he becomes a mother. Buddha is more like a mother than like a father. The Christian association with the word "father" is not very meaningful or beautiful. To call the divine "father" looks a little male-orientated. If there is a God it can only be a mother, not a father. "Father" is so institutional. A father is an institution. In nature, a father doesn't exist as such. If you ask a linguist he will say that the word "uncle" is older than the word "father." Uncles came first into existence because nobody knew who the father was. Once private property was fixed, once marriage became a form of private ownership, the institution of the father entered human life. It is very fragile, it can disappear any day. If the society changes, the institution can disappear as many other institutions have disappeared. But the mother is going to remain. The mother is natural.

In the East, many people, many traditions, have called God a mother. Their approach seems to be more relevant. Watch Buddha—his face seems more like a woman's face than like a man's. In fact, because of that we have not depicted him as having a beard or mustache. Mahavira, Buddha, Krishna, Ram—you never see any mustache or beard on their faces. Not that they were lacking in some hormones—they must have had beards—but we have not depicted them with beards because that would give their faces a more male-like appearance.

In the East we don't bother much about facts but we bother much about relevance, significance. Of course, the statues of Buddha that you have seen are all false, but in the East we don't worry about that. The significance is that Buddha has become more womanly, more feminine. It is a shift from the left hemisphere of the brain to the right hemisphere of the brain, from the male to the female, the shift from the aggressive to the passive, the shift from the positive to the negative, the shift from effort to effortlessness. Buddha is more feminine, more motherly. If you really become a meditator, by and by you will see many changes in your being and you will feel more like a woman than like a man—more graceful, more receptive, non-violent, loving. And a compassion will arise continuously from your being; it will be just a natural fragrance.

Ordinarily what you call compassion goes on hiding your passion in it. Even if you sometimes feel sympathetic towards people, watch, dissect it, go deeper into your feeling and somewhere you will find some motivation. In acts that look very compassionate, deep down you will always find some motivation.

I have heard:

Louie came back home. He was shocked to find his wife in the arms of another man. He rushed out of the room crying, "I am getting my shotgun."

His wife dashed after him despite her unclothed state, seized him and shouted, "You fool, what are you getting excited about? It was my lover who paid for the new furniture we recently got, my new clothes. The extra money you thought I earned sewing, the little luxuries we have been able to buy—they all came from him!"

But Louie wrenched away from her and continued upstairs.

"No shotgun, Louie!" yelled his wife.

"What shotgun?" called back Louie. "I'm getting a blanket. That poor fellow will catch cold, lying there naked like that."

Even if you feel—or you think you feel, or you pretend that you feel—compassion, just go deep and analyze it and you will always find some other motivation in it. It cannot be pure compassion. And if it is not pure, it is not compassion. Purity is a basic ingredient in compassion, otherwise it is something else—it is more or less a formality. We have learned how to be formal—how to behave with your wife, with your husband, how to behave with your children, with friends, with your family. We have learned everything. Compassion is not something which can be learned. When you have unlearned all formalities, all etiquette and manners, it arises in you. Compassion is wild; it doesn't taste of etiquette, of formality; they are all dead things compared to it. It is very alive, it is a flame of love.

At the twelfth hole of a hotly contested match, the grounds overlooked the highway and as Smith and Jones approached the green, they saw a funeral procession making its way along the road.

At this, Smith stopped, took off his hat, placed it over his heart, and bent his head till the procession disappeared around the bend.

Jones was astonished and after Smith had replaced his hat and returned to his game, he said, "That was delicate and respectful of you, Smith."

"Ah, well," said Smith, "I could not do less. I was married to the woman for twenty years, after all."

Life has become plastic, artificial, formal, because you have to do certain things that you do. You of course reluctantly follow duties, but if you miss much of life it is natural, because life is possible only if you are alive, intensely alive. If your own fame has become covered by formalities, duties, rules, which you have to fulfill reluctantly, you can only drag. You may drag comfortably, your life may be a life of convenience, but it cannot be really alive.

A really alive life is, in a way, chaotic. In a way, I say, because that chaos has its own discipline. It has no rules because it need not have any rules. It has the most basic rule in-built in it—it need not have any external rules.

Now a Zen story.

One winter day, a samurai came to Eisai's temple and made an appeal: "I'm poor and sick," he said, "and my family is dying of hunger. Please help us, master."

Dependent as he was on widows' mites, Eisai's life was very austere, and he had nothing to give. He was about to send the samurai off when he remembered the image of Yakushi-Buddha in the hall. Going up to it he tore off its halo and gave it to the samurai. "Sell this," said Eisai. "It should tide you over." The bewildered but desperate samurai took the halo and left.

"Master!" cried one of Eisai's disciples, "that's sacrilege! How could you do such a thing?"

"Sacrilege? Bah! I have merely put the Buddha's mind, which is full of love and mercy, to use, so to speak. Indeed, if he himself had heard that poor samurai he'd have cut off a limb for him."

A very simple story, but very significant. First, even when you have nothing to give, look again. You will always find something to give. It is a question of attitude. If you cannot give anything, at least you can smile; if you cannot give anything, at least you can sit with the person and hold their hand. It is not a question of giving some thing, it is a question of giving.

This Eisai was a poor monk as Buddhist monks are. His life was very austere and he had nothing to give. Ordinarily, it is an absolute sacrilege to take the halo off Buddha's statue and give it away. No so-called religious person could think of it. Only somebody who is *really* religious would do it—that's why I say compassion knows no rules, compassion is beyond rules. It is wild. It follows no formalities.

Then suddenly Eisai remembered the image of Buddha in the hall. In Japan, in China, they put a gold halo around the head of the Buddha, just to show the aura around his head. Suddenly Eisai remembered it—every day he must have worshipped the same statue.

Going up to it he tore off its halo and gave it to the samurai. "Sell this," said Eisai. "It should tide you over." The bewildered but desperate samurai took the halo and left.

Even the samurai was bewildered. He had not expected this. Even he must have thought that this was sacrilege. What type of man is this? He is a follower of Buddha and he has destroyed the statue! Even to touch the statue is sacrilege, and he has taken away the halo.

This is the difference between a real religious person and a so-called religious person. The so-called religious person always looks to the rule; he always thinks of what is proper and what is not proper.

But a really religious person lives it. There is nothing proper and improper for him. Compassion is so infinitely proper that whatsoever you do through compassion becomes proper automatically.

"Master!" cried one of Eisai's disciples, "that's sacrilege! How could you do such a thing?"

Even a disciple understands that this is not right. Something improper has been done.

"Sacrilege? Bah! I have merely put the Buddha's mind, which is full of love and mercy, to use, so to speak. Indeed, if he himself had heard that poor samurai he'd have cut off a limb for him."

To understand is something other than just to follow. When you follow, you become almost blind; then there are rules that have to be kept. If you understand, then too you follow but you are no longer blind. Each moment decides, each moment your consciousness responds, and whatever you do is right.

One of the most beautiful stories is about a Zen master who asked, one winter night, to be allowed to stay in a temple. He was shivering because the night was cold and snow was falling outside. Of course, the temple priest sympathized and told him, "You can stay, but only for the night, because this temple is not a hotel. In the morning you will have to go."

In the middle of the night the priest suddenly heard a noise. He came running and could not believe his eyes. The monk was sitting around a fire which he had made inside the temple. And one Buddha statue was missing. In Japan they make wooden Buddhas.

The priest asked, "Where is the statue?"

The master showed him the fire and he said, "It was very cold and I was shivering."

The priest said, "You seem to be mad! Don't you see what you have done? It was a Buddha statue. You have burnt Buddha!"

The master looked in the fire, which was disappearing, and poked the fire with a stick.

The priest asked, "What are you doing?"

He said, "I am trying to find the bones of the Buddha."

The priest said, "You are certainly mad. It is a wooden Buddha. There are no bones in it."

Then the master said, "The night is still long and it is getting even colder. Why not bring these two other Buddhas also?"

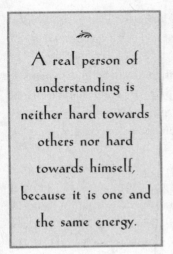

A real person of understanding is neither hard towards others nor hard towards himself, because it is one and the same energy.

Of course, he was thrown out of the temple immediately. This man was dangerous! As he was being thrown out he said, "What are you doing throwing a live Buddha out? For the sake of a wooden Buddha? The alive Buddha was suffering so much I had to show compassion. If Buddha were alive he would have done the same. He would himself have given all those three statues to me. I know it! I know from my very heart that he would have done the same."

But who was there to listen to him? He was thrown out into the snow and the doors were closed. In the morning, when the priest went out, he saw the master sitting near a milestone with a few flowers on top of it, worshipping it. The priest came again and said, "What are you doing now? Worshipping a milestone?"

The master said, "Whenever the time to pray comes, I create my Buddhas anywhere, because they are always all around. This milestone is as good as your wooden Buddhas inside."

It is a question of attitude. When you look with worshipful eyes, then anything becomes divine.

And remember—the story about Eisai is easy to understand because the compassion is shown towards somebody else. This story is even more difficult and complex to understand, because the compassion is shown towards oneself. A real person of under-standing is neither hard towards others nor hard towards himself, because it is one and the same energy. A real person of under-standing is not a masochist. He is not a sadist nor a masochist. A real person of understanding simply understands that there is no separation—all including himself is divine. And he lives out this understanding.

To live out of understanding is compassion. Never try to prac-tice it; simply relax deep into meditation. Be in a state of let-go in meditation, and suddenly you will be able to smell the fragrance that is coming from your own innermost depth. Then the flower blos-soms and compassion spreads. Meditation is the flower and compas-sion is its fragrance.

A DESIRE IS A DESIRE IS A DESIRE—
RESPONSES TO QUESTIONS

Will you please talk about the desire to help people, its differences and simi-larities to other forms of desire?

Desire is desire; there is no difference at all. Whether you want to help people or you want to harm people, the nature of desire re-mains the same.

A buddha does not desire to help people. He helps people, but there is no desire in it; it is spontaneous. It is just the fragrance of a flower that has bloomed. The flower is not desiring the fragrance to be released to people on the winds. Whether or not it reaches people is not the concern of the flower at all. If it reaches, that is accidental; if it does not reach, that too is accidental. The flower is sponta-neously releasing its fragrance. The sun rises—there is no desire to wake up people, no desire to open the flowers, no desire to help the birds to sing. It all happens of its own accord.

A buddha helps not because he desires to help but because compassion is his nature. Every meditator becomes compassionate, but not a "servant of the people." The servants of the people are mischievous; the world has suffered too much from these servants because their service is desire masquerading as compassion, and desire can never be compassionate.

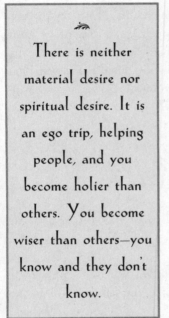

There is neither material desire nor spiritual desire. It is an ego trip, helping people, and you become holier than others. You become wiser than others—you know and they don't know.

Desire is always exploitation. You can exploit in the name of compassion; you can exploit with beautiful names. You can talk about service to humanity and about brotherhood, or about religion and God and truth. All your beautiful talk will bring only more and more wars, more and more bloodshed—more and more people will be crucified, burned alive. That's what has been happening up to now. And if you don't bring a new understanding to the world, it is going to continue in the same way.

So the first thing to be remembered is that to desire is the same, whether you desire to help or to harm. It is not a question of the object of desire; the question is of the nature of desire itself. The nature of desire leads you into the future; it brings the tomorrow in. And with the tomorrow come all the tensions, all the anxieties about whether you are going to make it or not, whether you are going to succeed or not. The fear of failure and the ambition to succeed will be there—whether you desire money or victory in the world, or you desire to be compassionate to people or to bring salvation to them, it is all the same game. Only names change. This is fundamental to understand.

A man asked Buddha, "I would like to help people. Instruct me." Buddha looked at him and became very sad. The man was puzzled, confused. He said, "Why have you become sad? Have I said anything wrong?"

Buddha said, "How can you help people? You have not even helped yourself! You will only harm them in the name of help."

First bring the light within your being. Let the flame be enkindled in your consciousness . . . and then you will never ask this question. Then, naturally, your very presence and whatever you do will be of great help.

Desire is desire. There is neither material desire nor spiritual desire. It is an ego trip, helping people, and you become holier than others. You become wiser than others—you know and they don't know. You want to help because you have arrived and they are all ignorant people stumbling in darkness, and you want to become a light for them. You want to become a master and you want to reduce them to disciples. If this desire is there, then this desire is not going to help them—and it is not going to help you, either. It will do double the harm. It is a double-edged sword; it will cut others and it will cut you too. It is destructive, it can't be creative.

Then there is another kind of help that is not coming out of desire, that is not growing out of any ego projection. That kind of help, that kind of compassion happens only at the ultimate peak of meditation, never before it. When the spring has come to your consciousness, when you are all flowers inside, fragrance starts reaching others. You need not desire it—in fact you can't help it. Even if you want to prevent it you can't prevent it. It is inevitable that it will reach to others. It will become a light in their life, it will be a herald of new beginnings—not because you are desiring it but because you are transformed.

There is a Buddhist meditation called Maitri Bhavana. *It starts by saying to oneself, "May I be well_ may I be happy, may I be free from enmity, may I be free from ill will against myself." After being penetrated by the feeling these thoughts generate, the next phase of the meditation consists in extending it to others—to start with, visualizing people you love and giving out this good feeling to them; then doing the same with people you love less, until you might even feel compassion for people you hate. I used to feel this meditation somehow opened me to others. But I dropped it because I saw in it the danger of it being some kind of self-hypnosis. I still feel attracted to this meditation but I am confused as to whether I should take it up again, maybe with a different attitude, or just drop it. Can you please speak about this meditation? I would be grateful.*

Maitri Bhavana is one of the most penetrating meditations. You need not be afraid of getting into some sort of self-hypnosis; it is not. In fact, it is a sort of de-hypnosis. It looks like hypnosis because it is the reverse process. It is as if you have come to see me from your home, you walked along the way, and now going back you will walk the same way. The only difference will be that now your back will be towards my house. The way will be the same, you will be the same, but your face was towards my house while you were coming; now your back will be towards my house.

Man is already hypnotized. It is not a question now of being hypnotized or not hypnotized—you are already hypnotized. The whole process of society is a sort of hypnosis. Somebody is told that he is a Christian, and it is so continuously repeated that his mind is conditioned and he thinks himself a Christian. Somebody is Hindu, somebody is a Mohammedan—these are all hypnoses. You are already hypnotized. If you think you are miserable, this is a hypnosis. If you think you have too many problems, this is a hypnosis. Whatsoever you are is a sort of hypnosis. The society has given you those ideas, and now you are full of those ideas and conditionings.

Maitri Bhavana is a de-hypnosis: it is an effort to bring back your natural mind; it is an effort to give you back your original face; it is an effort to bring you to the point where you were when you were born and the society had not yet corrupted you. When a child is born he is in *Maitri Bhavana*. *Maitri Bhavana* means a great feeling of friendship, love, compassion. When a child is born he knows no hatred, he knows only love. Love is intrinsic; hatred he will learn later on. Love is intrinsic; anger he will learn later on. Jealousy, possessiveness, envy he will learn later on. These will be the things the society will teach the child: how to be jealous, how to be full of hatred, how to be full of anger or violence. These things will be taught by the society.

When the child is born he is simple love. He has to be so, because he has not known anything else. In the mother's womb he has not come across any enemy. He has lived in deep love for nine months, surrounded by love, nourished by love. He knows nobody who is inimical to him. He knows only the mother and the mother's love. When he is born his whole experience is of love, so how can you expect him to know anything about hatred? This love he brings with himself; this is the original face. Then there will be trouble, then there will be many other experiences. He will start distrusting people. A newborn child is simply born with trust.

I have heard:

A man and a little boy entered a barber shop together. After the man received the full treatment—shave, shampoo, manicure, haircut, et cetera, he placed the boy in the chair.

"I'm going to buy a tie," the man said to the barber. "I will be back in a few minutes."

When the boy's haircut was completed and the man still had not returned, the barber said, "Looks like your daddy has forgotten all about you."

"That was not my daddy," said the boy. "He just walked up, took me by the hand and said, "Come on, son, we are gonna get a free haircut!"

Children are trusting, but by and by there will be experiences in which they will be deceived, in which they will get into trouble, in which they will be opposed, in which they will become afraid. By and by they will learn all the tricks of the world. That's what has happened to everybody, more or less.

Now, *Maitri Bhavana* is again creating the same situation: it is a de-hypnosis. It is an effort to drop hatred, anger, jealousy, envy, and come back to the world as you came in the first place. If you go on doing this meditation, first you start loving yourself—because you are closer to you than anybody else. Then you spread your love, your friendship, your compassion, your feeling, your well-wishing, your benediction, your blessings—you spread these to people you love, friends, lovers. Then, by and by, you spread these to more people that you don't love so much, then to people to whom you are indifferent— you neither love nor hate—then by and by to people you hate. Slowly you are de-hypnotizing yourself. Slowly you are again creating a womb of love around yourself.

When a buddha sits, he sits in existence as if the whole existence has again become his mother's womb. There is no enmity. He has attained to his original nature. He has come to know the essential in himself. Now you can even kill him but you cannot destroy his compassion. Even dying, he will remain full of compassion towards you. You can kill him but you cannot destroy his trust. Now he knows that trust is something so basic that once you lose trust you lose all. And if you don't lose trust and everything else is lost, nothing is lost. You can take everything from him but you cannot take his trust. *Maitri Bhavana* is beautiful; there is no need to drop it. It will be tremendously helpful. It is a de-structuring.

The ego is created with hate, enmity, struggle. If you want to drop the ego, you will have to create more love feelings. When you love, ego disappears. If you love tremendously and you love unconditionally and you love all, then the ego cannot exist. The ego is the most stupid thing that can happen to a man or to a woman. Once it has happened it is very difficult even to see it because it clouds your eyes.

I have heard:

Mulla Nasruddin and his two friends were talking about their resemblances. The first friend said, "My face resembles that of Winston Churchill. I have often been mistaken for him."

The second said, "In my case, people think I am Richard Nixon and ask me for my autograph."

Mulla said, "That's nothing. Well, in my case, I have been mistaken for God himself."

The first and second asked together, "How?"

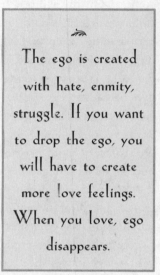

The ego is created with hate, enmity, struggle. If you want to drop the ego, you will have to create more love feelings. When you love, ego disappears.

Mulla Nasruddin said, "Well, when I was convicted and sent to jail for the fourth time, on seeing me the jailer exclaimed, 'Oh God, you have come again!'"

Once the ego has happened it goes on collecting from everywhere—sense, nonsense—but it goes on feeling itself important. In love you say "You are also important, not only I." When you love somebody, what are you saying? You may be speaking or not, but what is really deep in your heart? You are saying, whether in words or in silence, "You are also important, as much as I am." If love grows deeper, you will say, "You are even more important than me. If there arises a situation where only one can survive, I would die for you, and I would want you to survive." The other has become more important; you are even ready to sacrifice yourself for the one you love. And if this goes on spreading, as it goes on spreading in *Maitri Bhavana*, then by and by you start disappearing. Many moments will come when you will not be there—absolutely silent, not any ego at all, no center, just pure space. Buddha says, "When this is attained permanently, and you have become integrated to this pure space, then you are enlightened."

When the ego is lost completely you are enlightened; when you have become so egoless that you cannot even say "I am," you cannot even say that "I am a self." The word Buddha uses for that state is *anatta*: no-being, non-being, no-self. You cannot even utter the word "I," the very word becomes profane. In deep love, "I" disappears. You are de-structured.

When the child is born he comes without any "I." He simply is—a blank sheet, nothing is written on him. Now the society will start writing, and will start narrowing down his consciousness. The society will, by and by, fix a role for him—"This is your role; this is you"—and he will stick to that role. That role will never allow him to be happy because happiness is possible only when you are infinite. When you are narrow, you cannot be happy. Happiness is not a function of narrowness; happiness is a function of infinite space. When you are so spacious that the whole can enter into you, then only can you be happy.

Maitri Bhavana can be a tremendous help.

SHEEP'S CLOTHING—
WHAT COMPASSION
IS NOT

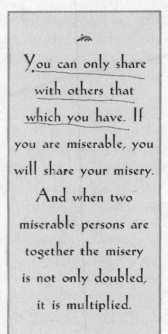

The blind cannot help the blind. Those who are groping in darkness cannot lead others to light. Those who don't know immortality cannot help others to drop the fear of death. Those who are not living totally and intensely, whose song is not yet of the heart, whose smile is only a painted smile on the lips, cannot help others to be authentic and sincere. Those who are hypocrites, pretenders, cannot help others to be honest.

Those who are not yet themselves, who know nothing about themselves, have no idea of their individuality—those who are still lost in their personality, which is fake and created by the society—cannot help anybody else to attain individuality. Even with all good intentions, it is simply not possible.

If your flame of life is not burning, how can you make the unlit lamps of others aflame? You have to be aflame;

You can only share with others that which you have. If you are miserable, you will share your misery. And when two miserable persons are together the misery is not only doubled, it is multiplied.

only then can you put others on fire. You have to be rebellious, then you can spread rebellion all around you. If you are on fire, aflame, you can create a wildfire that goes far beyond your vision. But first you have to be aflame.

The blind man leading another blind man . . . the mystic Kabir says both fall into the well. His original words are: *Andha andham thelia dono koop padant*: "The blind led the blind, and both have fallen into the well."

You have to have eyes to lead the blind to a physician—there is no other way. You can only share with others that which you have. If you are miserable, you will share your misery. And when two miserable persons are together the misery is not only doubled, it is multiplied. The same is true about your blissfulness, the same is true about your rebelliousness, the same is true about all experiences.

Whatever you want the world to be, you will have to be a model first. You have to pass through a fire test to prove your philosophy of life by your example. You cannot just go on arguing about it. Reasoning and argument will not help; only your experience can give to others the taste of love, of meditation, of silence, of religiousness.

Before you have experienced, never try to help anybody—because you will simply mess up the other person more. They are messed up already. Centuries of heritage have been messing up everybody. It will be very kind of you not to help, because it is going to be dangerous; your help will be very risky for the other person.

First travel the path, know perfectly well where it leads—only then can you hold the hands of others and take them on the path.

It is very difficult in this world to communicate. You have to learn how to communicate your experiences so that what reaches others is exactly what you want to say; otherwise you may be thinking of sharing nectar and it can turn into poison in their lives. They are poisoned enough already!

It is better to first cleanse yourself, make your eyes more transparent so that you can see better. Perhaps—then too, only perhaps—you may be able to help others. The desire is good, but good does not happen just from good desires.

The ancient saying is that the way to hell is paved with good intentions. There are millions of people who are helping with good intentions, advising others—not even bothering about the simple fact that they don't follow their own advice. But just the joy of advising is so much . . . who cares whether I follow my own advice or not?

The joy of advising others is a very subtle, egoistic joy. The person you are advising becomes ignorant; you become knowledgeable. Advice is the only thing in the world which everybody gives and nobody takes; and it is good that nobody takes it because it is given by people who know nothing—although there is no bad intention behind it.

Remember, in the very nature of things, if you want to change the world you have to change yourself first. The revolution must come to you first. Only then can you radiate it into others' hearts. First the dance must happen to you, and then you will see a miracle— others have started dancing, too.

The dance is contagious; so is love, so is gratitude, so is religiousness, so is rebellion—they are all contagious. But first you must have the flame that you want to see in others' eyes.

LOVING KINDNESS AND OTHER DELUSIONS OF GRANDEUR

Compassion is the ultimate flowering of consciousness. It is passion released of all darkness, it is passion freed from all bondage, it is passion purified of all poison. Passion becomes compassion. Passion is the seed, compassion is the flowering of it.

But compassion is not kindness, kindness is not compassion. Kindness is an ego-driven attitude, it strengthens your ego. When you are kind to somebody, you feel that you have the upper hand. When you are kind to somebody there is a deep insult behind it—you are humiliating the other and you are feeling happy in his humiliation. That's why kindness can never be forgiven. Whomsoever you have been kind to will remain somehow, somewhere, angry with you and is bound to take revenge. It is because kindness appears only on the surface as compassion, but in the depth it has nothing to do with compassion. It has other, ulterior motives.

Compassion is unmotivated—it has no motive at all. It is simply because you have, you give—not that the other needs. The other is not a consideration at all in compassion. Because you have so much, you go on overflowing. Compassion is spontaneous, natural, like breathing. Kindness is a cultivated attitude. Kindness is a kind of cunningness; it is calculation, it is arithmetic.

> You have heard, "Do unto others as you would have them do unto you." It is businesslike, it is not religious at all.

You have heard one of the most important sayings—it happens in almost all the scriptures of the world in one form or another—"Do unto others as you would have them do unto you." This is a calculated attitude, not compassion. This has nothing to do with religiousness—it is a very low kind of morality, a very worldly morality: "Do unto others as you would have them do unto you." It is businesslike, it is not religious at all. You are doing only because you would like exactly the same in return. It is selfish, it is self-centered, it is egoistic. You are not serving the other, you are not loving the other—in a roundabout way you are serving yourself. You are using the other. It is an enlightened egoism, but it is egoism—a very intelligent egoism, but it is egoism. Compassion is an uncalculated flowering, flowing. You simply go on giving because there is no other way to be.

So remember, the first thing: compassion is not kindness, in one sense—in the sense you use the word kindness it is not kindness. In another sense, compassion is the only real kindness. You are not "being kind" to somebody, you are not bigger than the other, you are simply releasing the energy that you are receiving from the whole. It comes from the whole and it goes back to the whole—you don't stand in the way as an obstacle, that's all.

When Alexander was traveling in India he went to see the great mystic Diogenes. Diogenes was lying down on a riverbank, taking a sunbath. Alexander had always cherished the desire to see this man Diogenes, because he had heard that this man had nothing, yet there is no other man who is more rich than this man. He has something within him, he was a luminous being. People said, "He is a beggar, but he is really an emperor." So Alexander had become intrigued. While traveling he heard that Diogenes was just nearby, so he went to see him.

Early morning, the sun is rising, Diogenes is lying naked on the sand . . . Alexander says, "I am happy to see you. Whatever I have heard seems to be true. I have never seen a happier man. Can I do something for you, sir?" And Diogenes said, "Just stand to the side—you are blocking the sun. And remember to never prevent the sun. You are dangerous, you can prevent the sun from reaching many people. Just stand to the side."

Compassion is not something that you give to others; it is simply not blocking the sun. See the point of it: it is simply not obstructing godliness. It is becoming a vehicle of the divine, it is simply allowing the divine to flow through you. You become a hollow bamboo and the divine goes on flowing through you. Only the hollow bamboo can become a flute, because only a hollow bamboo is capable of allowing a song to flow through it.

Compassion is not coming from you, compassion is from existence, from the divine. Kindness is coming from you—that's the first thing to be understood. Kindness is something that you do, compassion is something that existence does. You simply don't prevent it, you don't stand in the way. You allow the sun to fall, to penetrate, to go wherever it wants.

Kindness strengthens the ego, and compassion is possible only when the ego has disappeared utterly. So don't be misguided by your dictionaries, because in the dictionaries you will find compassion is synonymous with kindness. It is not so in the real dictionary of existence.

Zen has only one dictionary, the dictionary of the universe. Mohammedans have the Koran as their scripture, Hindus have the Veda, Sikhs have Gurugranth, Christians have the Bible, and Jews have the Talmud. If you ask me, "What is the scripture of Zen?" I would say they don't have any scripture, their scripture is the universe. That is the beauty of Zen. In every stone is the sermon, and in every sound of a bird God is reciting. In every movement around you it is existence itself dancing.

> Kindness is something that you do, compassion is something that existence does. You simply don't prevent it, you don't stand in the way.

Compassion is when you allow this eternal song to flow through you, to pulsate through you—when you co-operate with this divinity, when you move hand in hand with it. It has nothing to do with you; you have to disappear for it to be. For compassion to be, you have to disappear utterly—it can flow only into your absence.

Kindness cultivated makes you very egoistic. You can see it: people who are kind are very egoistic, more egoistic than the people who are cruel. This is strange—the cruel person at least feels a little guilty, but the so-called kind person feels perfectly okay, always holier-than-thou, always better than others. He is very self-conscious in what he is doing; each act of kindness brings more energy and more power to his ego. He is becoming greater and greater every day. The whole trip is of the ego.

This is the first thing to understand, that compassion is not the so-called kindness. It has the essential part of kindness in it—of being soft, of being sympathetic, of being empathetic, of not being hard, of being creative, of being helpful. But nothing is done as an act on your part; everything flows through you. It is from existence, and you are happy and thankful that existence has chosen you as a vehicle. You become transparent and kindness passes through you. You become a transparent glass so the sun passes through you—you don't hinder it. It is pure kindness with no ego in it.

The second thing is that compassion is not your so-called love either. It has the essential quality of love, but it is not what you know as love. Your love is just lust parading as love. Your love has nothing to do with love—it is a kind of exploitation of the other, in a beautiful name, with a great slogan.

You go on saying "I love you"—but have you ever loved anybody? You have simply used others; you have not loved. How can using the other be love? In fact, to use the other is the most destructive act possible in the world—because to use the other as a means is criminal.

Immanuel Kant, describing his concept of morality, says that to use the other as a means is immoral—the fundamental immoral act. Never use the other as a means, because everybody is an end unto himself. Respect the other as an end unto himself. When you respect the other as an end unto himself, you love. When you start using the other—the husband using the wife, the wife using the husband— there are motives. And you can see it all around.

People are not destroyed by hate, people are destroyed by their so-called love. And because they call it love, they can't look into it. Because they call it love they think it has to be good and all right. It is not. Humanity is suffering from this disease of so-called love; if you look deep down into it, you will find just naked lust. Lust is not love. Lust wants to get, love wants to give. The whole emphasis of lust is: "Get as much as you can, and give as little as you can. Give less, get more. If you have to give, give it only as bait." Lust is absolutely a bargain. Yes, you have to give something, because you want to get—but the idea is to get more and give less. That is what the business mind is. If you can get without giving, good! If you cannot get without giving, then give a little bit; pretend that you are giving much, and snatch the whole from the other.

Exploitation is what lust is. Love is not exploitation. So compassion is not love in the ordinary sense, and yet it is love in its real sense. Compassion only gives, it knows no idea of getting back. Not that it does not get back, no—never think that for a single moment. When you give without any idea of getting, you get back a thousandfold. But that is another thing; that has nothing to do with you. And when you want to get too much, in fact you are only deceived; you don't get anything. Finally, you are only disillusioned.

Each love affair ends in a disillusionment. Have you not observed it, that each love affair finally leaves you in a ditch of sadness, depression, with a sense of being cheated? Compassion knows no disillusionment because compassion does not start with an illusion. Compassion never asks for any return, there is no need. First, because the compassionate person feels, "It is not my energy that I am giving, it is the energy of existence itself. Who am I to ask anything in return for it? Even to ask for a thank you is meaningless."

That's what happened when a man came to Jesus, and Jesus touched him and he was cured. The man thanked Jesus—naturally, he was in tremendous gratitude. He had been suffering from that disease for years and there was no cure and the physicians had told him, "Now nothing can be done, you have to accept it." Now he is cured! But Jesus says, "No sir, don't be thankful towards me, be thankful towards God. It is something that has happened between you and God! I am nobody in it. It is your faith that has healed you, and it is God's energy that has become available because of your faith. I am, at the most, a bridge—a bridge through which God's energy and your faith have joined hands. You need not be concerned with me, you need not be thankful to me. Thank the divine, thank your own faith. Something has transpired between you and the divine. I come into it nowhere."

This is what compassion is. Compassion goes on giving, but knows no feeling of giving, knows no feeling that "I am the giver." And then existence goes on responding in thousands of ways. You give a little love and from everywhere love starts flowing. The man of compassion is not trying to snatch anything away, he is not greedy. He does not wait for the return, he goes on giving. He goes on getting too, but that is not in his mind.

So, the second thing is that compassion is not the so-called love, and yet it is the real love.

The third thing: Compassion is intelligence but not intellect. When intelligence is freed of all forms, of all logical forms, when intelligence is freed from all argumentation, when intelligence is freed from the so-called rationality, because rationality is a confinement—when intelligence is freedom, it is compassion. A man of compassion is tremendously intelligent, but he is not an intellectual. He can see through and through, he has absolute vision, he has real eyes to see, nothing is hidden to him—but it is

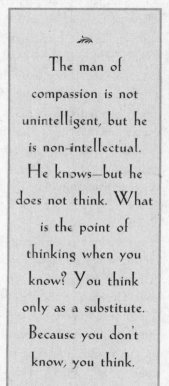

The man of compassion is not unintelligent, but he is non-intellectual. He knows—but he does not think. What is the point of thinking when you know? You think only as a substitute. Because you don't know, you think.

not guesswork. It is not through logic, it is not through inference, it is through clear eyesight.

Remember it: The man of compassion is not unintelligent, but he is non-intellectual. He is a tremendous intelligence, he is the very embodiment of intelligence. He is pure radiance. He knows—but he does not think. What is the point of thinking when you know? You think only as a substitute. Because you don't know, hence you think. Because you can't know, hence you think. Thinking is a substitute process—and it is a poor substitute, remember. When you can know, when you can see, who bothers to think?

The man of compassion knows; the intellectual thinks. The intellectual is a thinker and the man of compassion is a non-thinker, non-intellectual. Intelligence he has, tremendous intelligence he has, but his intelligence does not function through the pattern of intellect. His intelligence functions intuitively.

And the fourth thing: Compassion is not feeling—because feeling has many things in it which are not in compassion at all. Feeling has sentimentality, emotionality—those things don't exist in compassion. The man of compassion feels, but without any emotion. He feels, but there is no sentimentality. He will do whatever is needed, yet he remains untouched by it. This has to be understood very deeply. And once you understand compassion, you have understood what a buddha is.

Somebody is suffering—the man of feeling will start crying. Crying is not going to help. Somebody's house is on fire—the man of feeling will shout and cry and beat his chest. That is not going to help. The man of compassion will start moving! He will not cry, that is pointless; tears don't help. Tears cannot put the fire out, tears cannot become medicine for the suffering, tears cannot help a drowning man. A man is drowning and you are standing on the bank and crying and weeping—and crying and weeping really hard. You are a man of feeling, certainly, but not a man of compassion. The man of compassion immediately jumps into action. His action is immediate; he does not waver for a single moment. His action is instant—the moment something arises in his vision he immediately translates it into action. Not that *he* exactly translates—it is translated. His

understanding and his action are two aspects of the same phenomenon, they are not two separate things. One side of it is called understanding, the other side of it is called the act.

That's why I say a religious man is by his very nature involved,
committed—committed to life. He will not cry and weep. The man
of feeling sometimes appears as if he is the man of compassion. Don't
be misguided—the man of feeling is of no use. In fact he will create
more mess. He will not be of any help, he will create more confusion.
He will delay things rather than being a help.

The man of compassion is sharp. Without tears, without emotions, he simply moves into action. He is not cold, but neither is he
hot. He is simply warm—and cool. That is the paradox of the man of
compassion. He is warm because he is loving, and yet he keeps his
cool. His cool is never lost; whatsoever happens he remains cool, and
out of his coolness he acts. And because he remains cool, he helps.

These four things are to be understood, then you have a vision in
four dimensions of what compassion is. How does this compassion
arise?—because it cannot be cultivated. If you cultivate it, it becomes
kindness. How has this compassion to be brought into life? You cannot go into the scriptures, you cannot read and be helped by what
Buddha and Christ say, because that will bring the intellect in, it will
not bring intelligence. You cannot go on loving more and more, in the
way you have been loving up to now. If you move in the same direction you will not attain to compassion. Your love is not moving in the
right direction. If you go on loving in the same way—if you listen to
a buddha talking about love, or a christ talking about love, and you
think, "Good. So I have to love more, the way I have been loving up
to now," then your quantity will be more, but your quality will remain
the same. You will go in the same direction.

Your direction is basically wrong. You have not loved. Once this
thing sinks deep into your heart, that "I have not loved yet" . . . yes,
it is terrible to feel that "I have not loved yet"—it is very hard. We

can believe others have not loved—that's what we already believe—"nobody has loved me, that's okay, people are hard"—but to see that *you* have not loved shatters your ego.

That's why people don't want to see the simple fact that they have not loved yet. And because they don't want to see, they *don't* see. And because they don't see, they are never going to be transformed. They will go on moving in the same rut; they will go on repeating the same mechanical thing again and again And again and again they will be disillusioned.

So how to bring compassion in? If it were just your love you could have run in the same direction. To run faster, with more speed and more quantity, would be the right thing to do. But you are not moving in the right direction, so if you go faster, you will be going faster away from it, not towards it. Speed is not going to help, because in the first place you are moving in the wrong direction—it is the direction of lust and desire. Then how to bring compassion in? And I say it is not feeling either; otherwise you can cry your heart out, you can beat yourself, you can cry a thousand and one tears for a thousand and one sufferings all around, you can become very emotional. You can feel for everybody in Vietnam, in Korea, in Pakistan, or anywhere; you can feel for all the poor people.

Leo Tolstoy remembers his mother in his memoirs. He says she was a very kind woman, very kind—kind in the sense I have described it, not in the sense of compassion. She was very kind—so kind that she used to cry in the theater the whole time. They were rich people, they belonged to royalty. A servant used to be near Leo Tolstoy's mother with many handkerchiefs when she would go to the theater, because she would need them again and again. She was crying the whole time. And Tolstoy says, "But I was surprised to see that in Russia, even in winter when the cold would be so severe, below zero, with snow falling, she would go inside the theater and the driver of her coach would be sitting outside the coach, freezing in the falling snow, falling ill, even. She would never think about this man, who had to simply suffer and wait in the cold. But she would go on crying tears for something she had seen in the theater."

Sentimental people, emotional people—it costs nothing to cry, it costs nothing to feel. It costs much to be compassionate. It costs your whole life to be compassionate. A man of compassion is a very realistic man. The man of feeling simply lives in dreams, vague emotions, fantasies. So it cannot be brought through feeling, either. Then how to bring it? What is the Zen way to bring it? To bring it, the only way is meditation. It is attained through meditation. So we have to understand what meditation is.

Gautam Buddha, the founder of Zen, the founder of all great meditative techniques in the world, defines it in one word. Somebody asked him one day, "What is meditation? What is it all about?" And Gautam Buddha said a single word, he said: HALT! That was his definition of meditation. He says, "If it halts, it is meditation." The full sentence is: "The mad mind does not halt. If it halts, it is meditation."

The mad mind does not halt—if it halts, it is meditation. Meditation is a state of thoughtless awareness. Meditation is a state of non-emotional, non-sentimental, non-thinking awareness. When you are simply aware, when you become a pillar of awareness. When you are simply awakened, alert, attentive. When you are just a pure awareness.

How to enter into it? The Zen people have a special word for the entry, they call it *hua t'ou*. This Chinese word means ante-thought, or ante-word. The mind, before it is stirred by a thought, is called *hua t'ou*. Between two thoughts there is a gap; that gap is called *hua t'ou*.

Watch. One thought passes on the screen of your mind—on the radar screen of your mind one thought passes like a cloud. First it is vague—it is coming, it is coming—then it is there suddenly on the screen. Then it is moving, then it has gone out of the screen, again it becomes vague and disappears. . . . Another thought comes. Between these two thoughts there is a gap—for a single moment or a split second the screen is without any thought.

That state of pure no-thought is called *hua t'ou*—ante-words, ante-thought, before the mind is stirred. Because we are not alert inside, we go on missing it—otherwise meditation is happening each moment. You have just to see it happening, you have just to become aware what treasure you are carrying always within you. It is not that meditation has to be brought from somewhere else. The meditation is there, the seed is there. You have just to recognize it, nurture it, take care of it, and it starts growing.

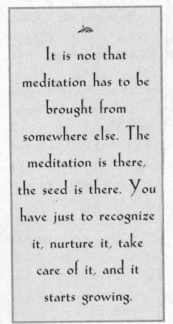

It is not that meditation has to be brought from somewhere else. The meditation is there, the seed is there. You have just to recognize it, nurture it, take care of it, and it starts growing.

The interval between two thoughts is *hua t'ou*. And that is the door to enter into meditation. *Hua t'ou*—the term literally means "word head." "Word" is a spoken word, and "head" is that which precedes the word. *Hua t'ou* is the moment before a thought arises. As soon as a thought arises it becomes a *hua wei*—*hua wei* literally means "word tail." And then, when the thought has gone or the word has gone and there is a gap again, it is again *hua t'ou*. Meditation is looking into this *hua t'ou*.

"One should not be afraid of rising thoughts," says Buddha, "but only of the delay in being aware of them." This is a tremendously new approach towards the mind, never attempted before Buddha. Buddha says one should not be afraid of rising thoughts.

One should only be afraid of one thing—of not being aware of them, of being delayed in awareness.

When a thought arises, if with the thought your awareness is also there—if you can see it arising, if you can see it coming, if you can see it there, if you can see it going—then there is no problem at all. This very seeing, by and by, becomes your citadel. This very awareness brings you many fruits. You can first see, when you see that you are not the thought. Thought is separate from you, you are not identified with it. You are consciousness and it is content. It comes and goes—it is a guest, you are the host. This is the first experience of meditation.

inimical to "I think therefore I am"

Zen talks about "foreign dust"—for instance, a traveler stops at an inn where he passes the night or takes his meal. Then he packs and continues his journey, because he has no time to stay longer. On the other hand, the host of the inn has nowhere to go. The one who does not stay is the guest, and the one who does stay is the host. Therefore, a thing is "foreign" when it does not stay. Or, on a clear day when the sun rises and sunlight enters the house through a window, the dust is seen moving in the rays of light—but the empty space is unmoving. That which is still is empty, and that which moves is dust. "Foreign dust" is the false thinking, and emptiness is your self-nature—the host who does not follow the guest in coming and going.

This is a great insight. Consciousness is not the content. You are consciousness: thoughts come and go, you are the host. Thoughts are the guests—they come and stay for a while, take a little rest, take food, or stay overnight, and then they are gone. You are always there. You are always the same, you never change—you are eternally there. You are eternity itself.

Watch it. Sometimes you are ill, sometimes you are healthy, sometimes you are depressed, sometimes you are happy. One day you were very small, a child, then you became a youth, and then you became old. One day you were strong; a day comes when you become weak. All these things come and go, but your consciousness remains the same. That's why, if you look inside, you cannot reckon how old you are—because there is no age. If you go inside and look and try to find out there how old you are, there is no age because there is no time. You are exactly the same as when you were a child or when you were a youth. You are absolutely the same inside. For age you have to look at the calendar, at the diary, at your birth certificate— you have to look for something outside. Inside you will not find any age or aging. Inside there is timelessness. You remain the same— whether there is a cloud called depression or a cloud called happiness, you remain the same.

Sometimes there are black clouds in the sky—the sky does not change because of those black clouds. And sometimes there are white clouds also, and the sky does not change because of those white clouds. Clouds come and go, and the sky remains. Clouds come and go, and the sky abides.

You are the sky and thoughts are the clouds. If you watch your thoughts minutely, if you don't miss them, if you look at them directly, the first thing will be this understanding—and this is a great understanding. This is the beginning of your buddhahood, this is the beginning of your awakening. You are no longer asleep, you are no longer identified with the clouds that come and go. Now you know that you abide forever. Suddenly all anxiety disappears. Nothing changes you, nothing will ever change you—so what is the point of being anxious, in anguish? What is the point of being worried? No worry can do anything to you. These things come and go, they are just ripples on the surface. Deep in your depth, not a single ripple ever arises. And you are there, and you are that. You are that being. Zen people call it the state of being a host.

Ordinarily, you have become too identified with the guests— hence your misery. One guest comes, you become too attached. And when the guest is packing and leaving, then you cry and you weep and you run around—and you go with him, at least to see him off, to give him a send-off. Then you come back crying and crying—one guest has left and you feel so miserable. Then another guest comes and again you fall in with the guest, again you become identified with the guest, and again he is going . . .

Guests come and go, they don't stay! They can't stay, they are not supposed to stay, they are not meant to stay.

Have you watched any thought? It never stays, it cannot stay. Even if you want to make it stay, it cannot. Try. That's what people try sometimes—they try to keep one word in the mind. For example, they want to keep one sound, *aum*, in the mind. For a few seconds they re-member and then it is gone, slipped away. Again they are thinking of their business, of the wife, of the children. . . . Suddenly they become aware—where is that *aum*? It has slipped out of the mind.

Guests are guests—they have not come to stay forever. Once you see that all that happens to you is going to move away from you, then why be worried? Watch: Let them be there, let them pack, let them leave. You remain. Can you see the peace that arises if you can feel that you always abide? This is silence. This is an unworried state. This is non-anguish. Suffering ceases the moment identification ceases. Don't get identified—that's all. And if you can watch some-body who lives in such eternal timelessness, you will feel a grace, a coolness, a beauty, around him.

It happened—the story is about Buddha, a beautiful story. Listen to it carefully, because you can miss it.

One day, at mealtime, the World Honored One put on his robe, took his bowl and entered the great town of Sravasti to beg for his food. After he had begged from door to door, he returned to his place. When he had taken his meal, he put away his robe and bowl, washed his feet, arranged his seat, and sat down.

Go slowly, as if the film is moving very slowly. It is a Buddha film, and Buddha films move very slowly. Again, let me repeat it . . .

*One day, at mealtime, the World Honored One put on his robe,
took his bowl and entered the great town of Sravasti to beg for his
food. After he had begged from door to door, he returned to his
place. When he had taken his meal, he put away his robe and bowl,
washed his feet, arranged his seat, and sat down.*

Visualize Buddha doing all this and then sitting down on his seat.

*This shows the Buddha's ordinary life and daily activities which
were similar to those of others and had nothing special about them.
There is, however, something which is uncommon, but very few
know it.*

What is that? What is that uncommon, unique quality?—because
Buddha is doing ordinary things. Washing his feet, arranging his seat,
sitting down, putting away his robe, putting away his bowl, going to
bed, coming back—ordinary things everybody is doing.

*. . . Subhuti, who was in the assembly, rose from his seat, uncov-
ered his right shoulder, knelt upon his right knee, respectfully joined
the palms of his hands and said to the Buddha: "It is very rare, O
World Honored One! It is very rare!"*

Now, nothing rare seems to be there on the surface. Buddha coming,
putting away his robe, putting away his bowl, arranging his seat,
washing his feet, sitting on the seat—there seems to be nothing un-
usual. And this man, Subhuti . . . Subhuti is one of the most insight-
ful disciples of Buddha—so many great and beautiful stories about
Buddha are concerned with Subhuti. This is one of those stories,
very rare.

*At the time, the elder Subhuti, who was in the assembly, rose from
his seat, uncovered his right shoulder, knelt upon his right knee,*

respectfully joined the palms of his hands and said to the Buddha: "It is very rare, O World Honored One, it is very rare!"

Never seen before, it is unique.

The Tathagata's daily activities were similar to those of other men but there was here one thing which was different, and those who sat face to face with him did not see it.

That day, suddenly Subhuti uncovered it, praised it, and said, "Very rare! Very rare!"

Alas! The Tathagata had been thirty years with his disciples and they still did not know anything about his common acts of daily life. As they did not know, they thought these acts were ordinary and let them pass unnoticed. They thought only that he was similar to others and were, therefore, suspicious of and did not believe what he said. Had Subhuti not seen clearly, no one would really know the Buddha.

So say the scriptures. If there had not been a Subhuti, nobody would have seen what was happening inside. What was happening inside? Buddha remains the host. Not for a single moment does he lose his eternity, timelessness. Buddha remains meditative. Not for a single moment does he lose his *hua t'ou*. Buddha remains in his *samadhi*—even when he is washing his feet, he is washing so alertly, so aware, so consciously. Knowing well that "These feet are not me." Knowing well that "This bowl is not me." Knowing well that "This robe is not me." Knowing well that "This hunger is not me." Knowing well that "All that is around me is not me. I am just a witness, a watcher of it all."

Hence the grace of Buddha, hence this unworldly beauty of Buddha, He remains cool. This coolness is what meditation is. It has to be attained by being more alert of the host, by being more alert of the guest, by getting disidentified with the guest, by disconnecting yourself from the guest. Thoughts come and go, feelings come and go, dreams come and go, moods come and go, climates change. All that changes is not you.

Is there something that remains unchanging? That's you. And that is godliness. And to know it, and to be it, and to be in it, is to attain to *samadhi*. Meditation is the method, *samadhi* is the goal. Meditation, *dhyana*, is the technique to destroy this identification with the guest. And *samadhi* is dissolving into the host, abiding in the host, getting centered there.

> *Each night one embraces a buddha while sleeping,*
> *Each morning one gets up again with him.*
> *When rising or sitting, both watch and follow one another.*
> *Whether speaking or not, both are in the same place.*
> *They never even for a moment part,*
> *But are like the body and its shadow.*
> *If you wish to know the buddha's whereabouts,*
> *In the sound of your own voice there is he.*

This is a Zen saying: "Each night one embraces a Buddha while sleeping." The Buddha is always there, the non-Buddha is also there. In you meet the world and nirvana, in you meet the immaterial and matter, in you meet the soul and the body. In you meet all the mysteries of existence—you are a meeting place, you are a crossroads. On one side the whole world, on the other side the whole of the otherworldly. You are just a link between the two. Now, it is only a question of emphasis. If you go on focusing yourself on the world, you remain in the world. If you start changing your focus, if you shift your focus and you start focusing on consciousness, you are a god. Just a small change, as if one changes a gear in the car—just like that.

"Each night one embraces a Buddha while sleeping, each morning one gets up again with him." He is always there, because consciousness is always there; not for a single moment is it lost.

"When rising or sitting, both watch and follow one another." The host and the guest, both are there. Guests go on changing, but somebody or other is always there in the inn. It is never empty—unless you become disidentified with the guest. Then an emptiness arises. Then sometimes it happens your inn is empty; there is only the host sitting at ease, not being bothered by any guests. Traffic stops, people don't come. Those moments are of beatitude, those moments are of great blessing.

"Whether speaking or not, both are in the same place." When you are speaking, there is also something silent in you. When you are lusting, there is something beyond lust. When you are desiring, there is somebody who is not desiring at all. Watch it, and you will find it. Yes, you are very close, and yet you are very different. You meet, and yet you don't meet. You meet like water and oil; the separation remains. The host comes very close to the guest. Sometimes they hold hands and hug each other, but still the host is the host and the guest is the guest. The guest is one who will come and go; the guest will go on changing. And the host is one who remains, who abides.

"They never even for a single moment part, but are like the body and its shadow. If you wish to know the Buddha's where-abouts, in the sound of your own voice there is he." Don't go on looking for the Buddha somewhere outside. He resides in you—he resides in you as the host.

Now, how to come to this state of the host? I would like to talk to you about a very ancient technique; this technique will be of tremendous help. To come to this unknowable host, to come to this ultimate mystery of your being, this is the way—one of the very simple ways Buddha has proposed:

Deprive yourself of all possible relationships, and see what you are.
Suppose you are not a son to your parents, nor the husband to your

wife, nor the father to your children, nor a relative to your kindred, nor a friend to your acquaintances, nor a citizen to your country, and so on and so forth—then you get you-in-yourself.

Just disconnect. Some time once a day, sit silently and disconnect yourself from all connections. Just as you disconnect the phone, disconnect yourself of all connections. Don't think anymore that you are a father to your sons—disconnect. You are no longer a father to your son, and you are no longer a son to your father. Disconnect from the idea that you are a husband or a wife; you are no longer a wife, no longer a husband. You are no longer a boss, no longer a servant. You are no longer black, no longer white. You are no longer Indian, Chinese, German. You are no longer young, no longer old. Disconnect, go on disconnecting.

A thousand and one connections are there—just go on disconnecting all the connections. When you have disconnected all the connections, then suddenly ask: Who am I? And no answer comes, because you have already disconnected all those answers that would have come.

"Who am I?" And an answer comes—"I am a doctor"—but you have disconnected from the patients. An answer comes—"I am a professor"—but you have disconnected yourself from your students. An answer comes—"I am Chinese"—but you have disconnected it. An answer comes—"I am a man" or "a woman"—but you have disconnected it. An answer comes—"I am an old person"—but you have disconnected it.

Disconnect all. Then you are in yourself. Then for the first time the host is alone and there is no guest. It is very good sometimes to be alone without any guest, because then you can see into your hostness more closely, more carefully. The guests create turmoil, the guests create noise, and they come and demand your attention. They say, "Do this, and hot water is needed, and where is the breakfast? And where is my bed? And there are bed bugs!" . . . and a thousand

and one things the guests bring, and the host starts running after the guests: "Yes, of course, you have to take care of these people!"

When you are completely disconnected, nobody bothers you—nobody *can* bother you. Suddenly you are there in all your aloneness—and that purity of aloneness, that pristine purity of aloneness. You are like virgin land, the virgin peak of a Himalaya where nobody has ever traveled.

This is what virginity is. This is what I mean when I say, "Yes, Jesus's mother was a virgin." This is what I mean. I don't agree with Christian theologians—whatever they say is all bull. This is what virginity is—Jesus must have been conceived by Mary when she was in such a disconnected state. When you are in such a disconnected state, of course if a child enters he can only be a Jesus, nobody else.

In ancient India there were methods for how to conceive a child. Unless you are tremendously in deep meditation, don't make love. Let meditation be a preparation for love: that is the whole meaning of tantra. Let meditation be the basis—only then make love. Then you invite greater souls. The deeper you are, the greater soul will be invited.

Mary must have been absolutely disconnected in that moment when Jesus penetrated her. She must have been in this virginity; she must have been a host. She was no longer a guest and she was no longer being harassed by the guest and no longer identified with the guest. She was not the body, she was not the mind, she was not her thoughts—she was not a wife, she was nobody. In this nobodiness she was there, sitting silently—a pure light, a flame without any smoke around it, a smokeless flame. She was virgin.

And I say to you, exactly the same is the case when Buddha is conceived or when Mahavira is conceived, or Krishna or Nanak—because these people cannot be conceived in any other way. These people can enter only the most virgin womb. But this is my meaning of being a virgin. It has nothing to do with the foolish ideas that go around—that she never made love to a man, that Jesus was not conceived with a man, that Jesus was not the son of Joseph. That's why Christians go on saying "Jesus the son of Mary." They don't talk about his father; he was not a father. "Son of Mary" and "Son of God"—there was no Joseph in between. But why be so angry towards poor Joseph? Why can't God use Joseph too, if he can use Mary? What is wrong in it? He uses Mary for the womb and that does not spoil the story; then why not use Joseph too? The womb is half the story, because one egg from the mother has been used; then why not use the sperm from Joseph? Why be so angry at this poor carpenter?

No, existence uses both. But the state of consciousness must have been of the host. And really, when you are the host there is no wonder if you receive a great guest—Jesus comes in! If you are disidentified from all the guests, then the divine becomes your guest. First you become the host, a pure host. Then the divine becomes your guest.

When you are disconnected you come to you-in-yourself. Now ask yourself: What is this "you-in-yourself"? You can never answer this question—it is unanswerable, because it is cut off from all knowable relationships. This way one stumbles upon the unknowable; this is entering into meditation. When you have become settled into it, utterly settled, it becomes enlightenment.

Now you will be able to understand this Zen story easily.

THE ZEN MASTER AND THE THIEF—A PARABLE OF FORGIVENESS

When Bankei held his seclusion-weeks of meditation, pupils from many parts of Japan came to attend. During one of these gatherings a pupil was caught stealing. The matter was reported to Bankei with the request that the culprit be expelled. Bankei ignored the case.

Later the pupil was caught in a similar act, and again Bankei disregarded the matter. This angered the other pupils, who drew up a petition asking for the dismissal of the thief, stating that otherwise they would leave in a body.

When Bankei had read the petition he called everyone before him. "You are wise brothers," he told them. "You know what is right and what is not right. You may go somewhere else to study if you wish, but this poor brother does not even know right from wrong. Who will teach him if I do not? I am going to keep him here even if all the rest of you leave."

A torrent of tears cleansed the face of the brother who had stolen. All desire to steal had vanished.

The story takes place in a meditation camp, a meditation session, so you have to understand what meditation is. That's why I went into meditation so deeply—otherwise you would miss the whole point of the story. These stories are not ordinary stories, they need a great background. Unless you understand what meditation is, you will read—"When Bankei held his seclusion-weeks of meditation"—but you will not understand.

. . . pupils from many parts of Japan came to attend. During one of these gatherings a pupil was caught stealing.

Those pupils are everywhere, because man is so money-minded. And don't think that the one who was stealing was very much different from those from whom he was stealing: they were all in the same boat. Both are money-minded. One has the money, one does not have the money—that is the difference. But both are money-minded.

The matter was reported to Bankei with the request that the culprit be expelled. Bankei ignored the case.

Why did he ignore the case? Because both are money-minded. Both are thieves—one thief trying to take things away from another thief, that's all. In this world, if you hoard something you become a thief, if you have something you become a thief. There are two kinds of thieves in the world: one, respectable thieves, recognized by the state, sanctioned, registered, licensed by the state—and another, unlicensed people doing it on their own. Illegal stealing and legal. The legal ones are the respected ones; the illegal ones of course are not respected, because they go against the rules.

Those people who are clever never go against the rules, they find ways to steal by getting around the rules. But there are a few people who are not so clever. Seeing that if they follow these rules they will never have anything, they drop the rules and start doing illegal things. But everybody is a money maniac. That's why Bankei ignored the case.

Later the pupil was caught in a similar act, and again Bankei disregarded the matter.

He knows that both are in the same boat; there is not much difference.

You will be surprised to know that when a man succeeds in his criminal acts, he becomes respectable. Only if he fails, then he becomes a criminal. The successful robbers become kings, and the unsuccessful kings become robbers. It is only a question of who succeeds. If you are powerful, you are a great emperor. Now what is this Alexander, the great Alexander? A great robber—but he succeeded.

Your so-called politicians are all robbers. They try to destroy other robbers—they may be against smuggling, they may be against thievery, they may be against this and that. But deep down they are the greatest smugglers, the greatest thieves. But they do things legally—or at least they manage to show that they are doing things legally. And they succeed, at least while they are in power. When the power goes, then all those beautiful stories about them simply disappear.

Once a politician is deposed, he becomes an ugly phenomenon. He may be a Richard Nixon or she may be an Indira Gandhi. Once a politician is deposed, once the power is gone, once the power is no longer there to protect you, then everything is exposed. If you know how a person has become rich then you will not be able to respect him. But if the person is really rich he can manage to keep people silent. And then people have a very small memory—they forget.

I was reading in some history book that twenty persons were expelled from England; they were sea pirates. And what happened after thirty years? Of all those twenty persons, a few of them went to Australia, and a few of them went to America. A few of them had become governors in America, a few of them had become bankers, landlords—all twenty had become very respectable people.

That's why Bankei ignored the situation. He didn't pay much attention, he didn't take any note of it. "It's okay, this is how things go in the world." One who is not money-minded will ignore it.

This angered the other pupils, who drew up a petition asking for the dismissal of the thief, stating that otherwise they would leave in a body.

Now, these people were not there to meditate at all. If you have come to meditate, you understand a few requirements—that you have to grow into less money-mindedness, that you have to attain a certain detachedness from all your possessions. That it does not matter much that somebody has taken a few rupees—that it doesn't matter much, that it is not such a life-and-death affair. That you have to understand how the mind functions, how people are money-minded.

You are against the thief because he has taken your money. But how was it yours? You must have taken it from somebody else in some other way—because nobody comes with money into the world, we all come empty-handed. All that we possess we claim as our own, but nothing belongs to anybody. If a person has really come to meditate, this will be his attitude—that nothing belongs to anybody. He has less and less attachment to things.

But these people were money-minded. And when you are money-minded, naturally politics comes in. When they saw that the thief had been ignored twice, they must have thought, "What kind of master is this? It seems he is in favor of the thief!" They could not understand why he was ignoring it. He is ignoring it just to show them that they have to drop their money-mindedness. Yes, stealing is bad, but their money-mindedness is not good either.

When they saw that twice they had been ignored, they grew angry. They drew up a petition—politics comes in immediately, protest, petition—"asking for the dismissal of the thief, stating that otherwise they would leave in a body."

Now, they were not there to meditate at all. If they were really there to meditate, their approach towards this problem would have been totally different. They would have felt a little more compassion for this man, for his lust for money. If they were real meditators they would have contributed some money and given it to this man—"You please keep this money, rather than stealing." That would have been an indication that they were there to meditate, to be transformed.

But now they draw up a petition asking for the dismissal of the thief. Not only that—with a threat that if he is not thrown out they will leave in a body.

You cannot threaten a master like Bankei.

When Bankei had read the petition he called everyone before him. "You are wise brothers," he told them. "You know what is right and what is not right. You may go somewhere else to study if you wish, but this poor brother does not even know right from wrong. Who will teach him if I do not? I'm going to keep him here even if all the rest of you leave."

Many things have to be understood. When the master says, "You are wise brothers," he is ridiculing them, he is simply hitting them hard. He is not saying they are wise, he is saying they are utter fools. But all fools think themselves wise. In fact, to think oneself wise is one of the basic requirements of being a fool. Wise people think they are not wise. Foolish people always think they are wise.

Now, these are all fools. They were not there to possess money, they were not there to get money—they were there to get something greater, something far higher, but they have forgotten all about it. In fact, this man has given them an opportunity to see. If they were real meditators they would have gone to this man and thanked him—"You have given us an opportunity to see how much we cling to money. How much you have disturbed us! We have completely forgotten all about meditation, we have forgotten for what we have come. We have forgotten this master Bankei."

They may have traveled for hundreds of miles. They must have traveled for months, because in those days travel was not so easy. They had come, they had heard about this master and they had come from faraway places to study meditation with him. And somebody steals, and they have forgotten all! They should have thanked the thief: "You have brought something into our consciousness—some mad attachment to money has bubbled up, has surfaced."

When Bankei says, "You are wise brothers," he is joking. He is saying, "You are utter fools. But you think you are very wise, you think you know what is right and what is wrong. You have even been trying to teach *me* what is right and what is wrong. You are telling me, 'You throw this man out, otherwise we will leave.' You are trying to dictate terms to me. You think you know what is right and what is wrong? Then you can go anywhere—because you are so wise, you will be able to learn anywhere. But where will this man go? He is such a fool!"

> Life is so complex and life is so subtle that you cannot decide so easily that you are right and somebody else is wrong. In fact, one who has a little understanding will see that he never falls into the trap of being righteous.

See the point, the irony of it. Remember, the righteousness of the righteous is never very right. The people who think they are right are almost all stupid people. Life is so complex and life is so subtle that you cannot decide so easily that you are right and somebody else is wrong, In fact, a man who has a little understanding will see that he never falls into the trap of being righteous.

Now these pupils of Bankei think they know what is right and what is wrong, and this thief has committed wrong, and the master should throw him out. And if the master does not throw him out, then the master is also wrong. Now they are too much into their wisdom—they think they know. They don't see the master's compassion, they don't see the master's meditation. They don't see that the master has become a buddha—Bankei is one of the great masters of Zen. They don't see who is present before them, and they are protesting and threatening him.

Man is so foolish—he has done all kinds of foolish things down the ages. And the most foolish things have been committed whenever there is a buddha—because you cannot understand, you cannot see who is confronting you. You go on in your childish and juvenile ways; you go on talking nonsense.

Bankei says:

You are wise brothers, you know what is right and what is not right. You may go somewhere else to study if you wish, but this poor brother does not even know right from wrong. Who will teach him if I do not?

So you go, and I will keep him and I will teach him.

I am going to keep him here even if all the rest of you leave.

Sometimes it happens that the one who thinks he is right is more difficult to teach than the one who thinks that he is not right. It is easier to teach a criminal than to teach a saint. It is easier to teach a man who feels deep down that he is doing something wrong—because he is ready to learn. He himself wants to get rid of this state. But a man who thinks "I am doing right"—he does not want to get rid of this state, he is perfectly happy with it. It is impossible to change him.

Why does the master say, "You all can go and I am going to keep this one man, this poor brother"? Why? Because this poor brother has a possibility, a potentiality.

It happened that one man, a great criminal, murderer, a sinner, came to be initiated by Buddha. When he came he was afraid that people might not allow him entry; the disciples might not allow him to see Buddha. So he came at such a time when there were not too many people. And he didn't enter from the main gate, he jumped over a wall.

By chance Buddha was not there—he had gone begging—and the man was caught. He said to the disciples, "I have not come to steal or anything, I was just afraid that you wouldn't allow me through the main gate. Everybody knows me, I am a well-known figure around here. I am the most hated and feared person around here, everybody knows me. So I was afraid you might not allow me, you might not believe that I want to become a disciple."

So they took the man to one of Buddha's great disciples, Sariputra—who was an astrologer too, and had a capacity, a telepathic capacity, to read people's past lives. They asked Sariputra, "Look into this man. We know that in this life he is a murderer, a sinner, a thief, and he has done all kinds of things. But maybe he has earned some virtue in his past lives—maybe that's why he wants to become a sannyasin. Just look into his past lives."

Sariputra looked into his eighty thousand past lives . . . and he had always been the same! Even Sariputra started trembling, seeing this man. He is so dangerous—eighty thousand times a murderer, a criminal, always a sinner. He is an *established* sinner! It is impossible—any change in this man is not possible. Even Buddha cannot do anything.

Sariputra said, "Throw this man out, take him away immediately—because even Buddha will be a failure with this man. He is an established sinner. Just as Buddha is an established buddha, he is an established sinner. Eighty thousand lives I have seen, and I cannot go beyond that. Enough is enough!"

So the man was turned out. He felt so hurt, that there was no chance for him. Alive, he could not be around Buddha—so he wanted to commit suicide. Just around the corner from the main gate he went to the wall and was going to hit his head against the stone wall to kill himself. And suddenly Buddha comes back after his begging rounds, and sees that man. He stops him, and he takes him inside and he initiates him.

And the story says that within seven days the man became an *arhat*—within seven days he became an enlightened man. Now, everybody was very puzzled. Sariputra went to Buddha and he said, "What is this? Is all my clairvoyance, all my astrology just nonsense? I looked into this man's eighty thousand lives! If this man can become enlightened in seven days, then what is the point of looking into people's past lives? Then it is all absurd. How can such a thing happen?"

And Buddha said, "You looked into his past, but you didn't look into his future. And the past is past! Any moment a person decides to change, he can change—the very decision is decisive. And when a man has lived eighty thousand lives of misery, he knows—and he hankers to change, and his intensity of purpose to change is infinite. Hence, in seven days it can happen.

"Sariputra, you have not yet become enlightened. You are a good man, you have good lives—you don't feel so burdened with your past. You have a kind of righteousness around yourself. You have been a Brahmin for many lives, a scholar, a respected person. But look at this man. He was burdened in all those eighty thousand lives, and he wanted to get free. He really wanted to get free; hence the miracle—within seven days he is out of the prison. The intensity of his past was driving him."

This is one of the basic things to understand in people's transformation. People who feel guilty are easily transformed. People who feel good, right, are very difficult to transform. Religious people are very difficult to transform, irreligious people are easier to transform.

So whenever a religious person comes to me I don't take much note of him. But whenever an irreligious person comes to me I'm really interested. I'm into him, I am with him, I am all for him because there is a possibility.

That's why Bankei says:

"Who will teach him if I do not? I am going to keep him here even if all the rest of you leave."

A torrent of tears cleansed the face of the brother who had stolen. All desire to steal had vanished.

And in that shower of compassion from the master, the thief is no longer a thief, he is utterly cleansed. He started crying, and those tears cleansed his heart. *A torrent of tears cleansed the face of the brother who had stolen, and all desire to steal had vanished.* This is the miracle of the presence of a master. And the story does not say anything about what happened to all those political people.

This is the mystery of life. Never feel righteous, and never pretend that you are right—never get hooked into that idea. And never think about somebody else that he is wrong, because both those things go together—if you feel yourself right, you are always condemning others and thinking somebody else is wrong. Never condemn anybody, and never go on praising yourself; otherwise you will miss. Accept however people are. That is the way they are, and who are you to decide whether they are right or wrong? If they are wrong they suffer, if they are right they are blessed. But who are you to condemn them?

Your condemnation brings a certain ego in you. That's why people talk so much about others' wrongness—it gives a feeling that they are right. Somebody is a murderer, and they have a good feeling: "I am not a murderer—at least I am not a murderer." Somebody is a thief, and they feel good: "I am not a thief." And so on, so forth, their ego goes on strengthening. People talk about others' sins and about others' crime and all the wrong that goes on in others' lives. People go on talking about it. They exaggerate it, and they enjoy it—it all gives them a feeling that "I am good." But this feeling will become the barrier.

Be compassionate, be intelligent, be loving. Look at others with no judgment. And never start feeling righteous, never start feeling a kind of holiness. Never become a "His Holiness" or "Her Holiness." Never.

Remain ordinary, remain nobody. And in your nobodiness comes the ultimate guest . . . in your nobodiness you become the host.

HEARTS AND MINDS—RESPONSES TO QUESTIONS

What does it mean to try and help another person? Often, it seems more like trying to change them than to respect and love them unconditionally. Can you speak about this?

There is a vast difference, and tremendously significant, between trying to change the other and helping him. When you help somebody you help him to be himself; when you try to change somebody you try to change him according to your idea. When you try to change somebody you try to make him into a carbon copy. You are not interested in the person; you have a certain ideology, a fixed idea, an ideal, and you try to change the person according to the ideal. The ideal is more important, the real human being is not important at all.

In fact, trying to change the other according to some ideal is violent. It is aggression, it is an effort to destroy the other. It is not love, it is not compassion. Compassion always allows the other to be himself. Compassion has no ideology, compassion is just a climate. It does not give you direction, it only gives you energy. Then you move. Then your seed has to sprout according to its own nature. There is nobody forcing anything on you.

When I say, "Go and help others," I mean help them to be

themselves. When I say the world is irreligious because of so many preachers, I mean that too many people are trying to change, convert, transform others according to their own ideology. The idea should not be more important than the person. Even the whole of humanity is not more important than a single human being. Humanity is an idea; a single human being is a reality.

Forget about humanity, remember the human being—the real, the concrete, the throbbing, the alive. It is very easy to sacrifice human beings for humanity. It is very easy to sacrifice human beings for Islam, Christianity, Hinduism; it is very easy to sacrifice them for the idea of Christ, Buddha. Help, but don't sacrifice. Who are you to sacrifice anybody? Each individual is his own end. Don't use him as a means.

That is the meaning when Jesus says, "The Sabbath is made for man, not man for the Sabbath." Everything is made for man; man is the supreme value. Even the idea of God is for man; man is not for the idea of God. Sacrifice everything to man and don't sacrifice man to anything whatsoever. Then you help.

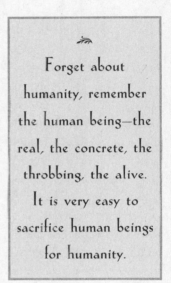

Forget about humanity, remember the human being—the real, the concrete, the throbbing, the alive. It is very easy to sacrifice human beings for humanity.

If you start sacrificing the human being, then you are not helping. You are destroying, you are crippling the other. You are violent, you are a criminal. So all your so-called religious teachers who try to change the other are criminals. One can just love, help, be ready to give unconditionally.

Share your being, but let the other move towards his or her own destiny. That destiny is unknown; nobody knows what is going to flower. Don't give a pattern, otherwise the flower will be crushed.

And remember that each individual being is unique. There has never been such a being before and there is never going to be again. Existence never repeats, it is not repetitive. It goes on inventing.

If you are trying to make a man be like Jesus, you will be destructive. Jesus can never be repeated. And there is no need! One is beautiful, many will just be boring. Don't try to make a person a buddha. Let him become himself; that is his buddhahood. And neither do you know nor does he know what he is carrying within himself. Only the future will show what it is. Not only will you be surprised; the person himself will be surprised when his flower opens. Everybody is carrying a flower of infinite potentiality and power, of infinite possibility.

You can, authentically, only be yourself. All else will be false, all else will be just masks, personalities, but not your essence.

Help, give energy, love. Accept the other and give him a feeling that he is welcome. Don't give him a feeling of guilt, don't give him the idea that he is condemned. All those who are trying to change him give him a feeling of guilt, and guilt is poison.

When somebody says, "Be like Jesus!" he has denied you as you are. Whenever somebody says to be like somebody else, you are not accepted. You are not welcome, you are like an intruder. Unless you become somebody else, you will not be loved. What type of love is this, which destroys you, and only when you become false, inauthentic?

You can, authentically, only be yourself. All else will be false, all else will be just masks, personalities, but not your essence. You can decorate yourself with the personality of Buddha, but it will never touch your heart. It will never be related to you, it will not be connected with you. It will just be on the outside. A face, but never your face.

So whoever is trying to make you somebody else and says, "I will love you if you become like Buddha, like Christ . . ." does not love you. He may be in love with Christ, but he hates you. And his love for Christ can also not be very deep, because if he has really loved Jesus, he would understand the absolute uniqueness of every individual.

Love is a deep understanding. If you have loved one person, you have triggered a different quality of vision within you. Now you can see with clarity. If you have loved Jesus, then whoever comes before you, you will see the reality of this person, of this concrete human being, of this potentiality here and now. And you will love this person, you will help this person to become whatsoever he or she can become. You will not expect anything else. All expectation is condemning, all expectation is a denial, all expectation is a rejection. You will simply give your love—for no reward, for no result. You will simply help, with no future in mind.

When love flows without any future, it is a tremendous energy. When love flows without motivation it helps, and nothing helps like it. Once you feel that even one single human being accepts you as you are, you feel centered. You are not unwelcome in this existence. At least one human being accepts you unconditionally. That gives you a grounding, a centering; that gives you a feeling that you are at home. When you are far away from yourself, you are far away from existence, from your home. The distance between you and yourself is the distance between you and your home, and there is no other distance. So whosoever says, "Become somebody else," is pushing you away from your home. You will become false, you will carry masks. You will have personalities, character, and a thousand other things, but you won't have a soul; you won't have the essential. You will not be an awareness, you will be a deception: a pseudo phenomenon, not authentic.

So when I say help, I'm saying just create a climate around people. Wherever you move, carry the climate of love and compassion, and help the other to be himself or herself.

That is the most difficult thing in the world—to help the other to be himself—because that is against your ego. Your ego would like to make imitators of people. You would like everybody to imitate you; you would like to become the archetype and have everybody follow you. Then your ego would be very, very fulfilled. You would think of yourself as the blueprint and everybody just has to follow you. You become the center and everybody becomes false.

No, the ego will not like the idea. It wants to change others according to you. But who are you to change anybody? Don't take that responsibility. That is dangerous; that is how Adolf Hitlers are born. They take the responsibility of changing the whole world according to themselves.

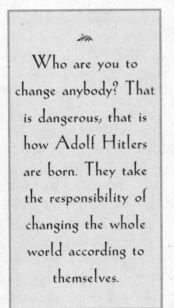

Who are you to change anybody? That is dangerous, that is how Adolf Hitlers are born. They take the responsibility of changing the whole world according to themselves.

There is much difference on the surface between a Mahatma Gandhi and an Adolf Hitler. But deep down there is no difference at all, because both have ideas of changing the world according to themselves. One may be using violent methods, the other may be using nonviolent methods, but both are using methods to change the other according to themselves. One may be using the bayonet, the other is threatening you that "I will go on a long fast if you don't follow me." One may be threatening to kill you and the other may be threatening that he will kill himself if he is not followed, but both are using force. Both are creating situations in which you can be forced to be something that you don't want to be, that you never wanted to be. They are both politicians. Neither Hitler loves you, nor Gandhi loves you. Gandhi talks about love, but he does not love. He cannot love, because the very idea—the ideal of how you should be—creates trouble.

There is only one way of loving people and that is to love them as they are. And this is the beauty: that when you love them as they are, they change. Not according to you—they change according to their own reality. When you love them, they are transformed. Not converted—transformed. They become new, they attain new heights of being. But that happens in their being, and it happens according to their nature.

Help people to be natural, help people to be free, help people to be themselves, and never try to force anybody, to pull and push and manipulate. Those are the ways of the ego. And that is what all politics is.

When does caring for another person become an interference in their life?

The moment ideology enters, care becomes interference. Love turns bitter, becomes almost a kind of hatred, and your protection becomes a prison. The ideology makes the difference.

For example, if you are a mother, take care of the child. The child needs you, cannot survive without you. You are a must. He needs food, he needs love, he needs care—but he does not need your ideology. He does not need your ideals. He does not need your Christianity, your Hinduism, your Islam, your Buddhism. He does not need your scriptures, he does not need your beliefs. He does not need your ideals of how he should be. Only avoid ideology, ideals, goals, ends—and then care is beautiful, then care is innocent. Otherwise care is cunning.

When there is no ideology in your caring—you don't want to make your child a Christian, you don't want to make your child this or that, communist or fascist, you don't want your child to become a businessman or a doctor or an engineer . . . . You don't have any ideas for your child. You say, "I will love, and when you grow up, you choose. Be whatever is natural for you to be. Whatever you are, you have my blessings and whatever you decide to be, from my side you are accepted and welcome. Not that only when you become the president of the country will I love you and if you become just a carpenter then there will be no love and I will feel ashamed of you. Not that only when you bring a gold medal from the university will there be a welcome, and if you come back a failure I will be ashamed of you. Not that only when you are good, virtuous, moral, this and that, will you be my child and otherwise I am not related to you, you are not related to me."

The moment you bring any idea, you bring poison into the relationship. Care is beautiful, but when care has some idea behind it, then it is cunningness. Then it is a bargain, then it has conditions. And all our love is cunning; hence this misery in the world, this hell. Not that there is no care—care is there, but with too much cunningness. The mother cares, the father cares, the husband cares, the wife cares, the brother, the sister—everybody is caring, I'm not saying that nobody is caring. People are caring so much, but still the world is hell. Something is wrong, something is fundamentally wrong.

> Have you ever loved anybody as he or she is? You don't want to improve the person, you don't want to change them; your acceptance is total, utter—then you know what care is.

What is that fundamental wrong? Where do things go wrong? The caring has conditions in it: "Do this! Be that!" Have you ever loved anybody with no conditions? Have you ever loved anybody as he or she is? You don't want to improve the person, you don't want to change them; your acceptance is total, utter—then you know what care is. You will be fulfilled through that care, and the other will be helped immensely.

And remember, if your care has no business in it, no ambitions in it, the person you cared about will love you forever. But if your care has some ideas in it, then the person you cared about will never be able to forgive you. That's why children are incapable of forgiving their parents. Go and ask the psychologists, the psychoanalysts—almost all the cases that come to them are those whose parents cared too much when they were children. And their care was businesslike; it was cold, it was calculated. They wanted some of their ambitions to be fulfilled through the child.

Love has to be a free gift. The moment there is a price tag on it, it is no longer love.

COMPASSION IN
ACTION

❧

Nobody can be unselfish—except hypocrites.

The word "selfish" has taken a very condemnatory association, because all the religions have condemned it. They want you to be unselfish. But why? To help others . . .

I am reminded: A small child was talking to his mother, and the mother said, "Remember always to help others." And the child asked, "Then what will the others do?" Naturally the mother said, "They will help others." The child said, "This seems to be a strange scheme. Why not help yourself, rather than shifting it and making things unnecessarily complex?"

Selfishness is natural. Yes, there comes a moment when you are sharing by being selfish. When you are in a state of overflowing joy, then you can share. Right now miserable people are helping other miserable people, the blind leading others who are blind. What help can you give? It is a very dangerous idea which has prevailed throughout the centuries.

In a small school the lady teacher told the boys, "At least once per week you should do a good thing." One boy asked, "Just please give us some examples of good things. We don't know what is good." So she said, "For example, a blind woman wants to cross the street; then help her to cross the street. This is a good job; this is virtuous."

The next week she asked, "Did any of you remember to do what I have said to you?" Three children raised their hands. She said, "This is not good—the whole class has not been following. But still, it is good that at least three boys did something good." She asked the first, "What have you done?" He said, "Exactly what you have said: One old woman who was blind, I helped her to cross the street."

She said, "That's very good. God will bless you." She asked the second, "What have you done?" He said, "The same—a blind old woman, I helped her to cross the street." The teacher became a little puzzled—where are they finding blind old women? But it is a big city; perhaps they may have found two. She asked the third and he said, "I did exactly what they have done: helped a blind old woman cross the street."

The teacher said, "But where did you find three blind women?" They said, "You don't understand: there were not three blind women, there was only one blind woman. And it was so hard to help her to cross the street! She was beating us and shouting and screaming, because she did not want to cross, but we were intent on doing some virtuous act. A crowd gathered, people were shouting at us, but we said, 'Don't be worried. We are taking her to the other side.' But she never wanted to go to the other side!"

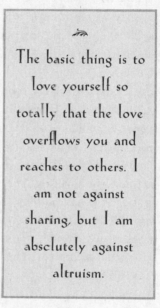

The basic thing is to love yourself so totally that the love overflows you and reaches to others. I am not against sharing, but I am absolutely against altruism.

People are being told to help others, and they are empty within themselves. They are being told to love others—love your neighbors, love your enemies—and they are never told to love themselves. All the religions, directly or indirectly, are telling people to hate themselves. A person who hates himself cannot love anybody; he can only pretend.

The basic thing is to love yourself so totally that the love over-flows you and reaches to others. I am not against sharing, but I am ab-solutely against altruism. I am for sharing, but first you must have something to share. And then you are not doing anything as an obliga-tion to anybody—on the contrary, the person who receives something from you is obliging you. You should be thankful, because the other could have rejected your help; the other has been generous.

My whole insistence is that the individual should be so happy, so blissful, so silent, so content, that out of his state of fulfillment he starts sharing. He has so much, he is like a rain cloud: he has to shower.

If others' thirst is quenched, if the thirst of the earth is quenched, that is secondary. If each individual is full of joy, full of light, full of silence, he will be sharing it without anyone telling him, because shar-ing is such a joy. Giving it to someone is more joyful than getting it.

But the whole structure should be changed. People should not be told to be altruistic. They are miserable—what can they do? They are blind—what can they do? They have missed their life—what can they do? They can give only what they have got. So people are giv-ing misery, suffering, anguish, anxiety to everybody else that comes in contact with them. This is altruism! No, I would like everybody to be utterly selfish.

Each tree is selfish: it brings water to its roots, it brings juices to its branches, to the leaves, to the fruits, to the flowers. And when it blossoms, it releases fragrance to everybody: known, unknown; fa-miliar, stranger. When it is loaded with fruits, it shares, it gives those fruits. But if you teach these trees to be altruistic, all these trees will die, just as the whole humanity is dead—just corpses walking. And walking to where? Walking to their graveyard, finally to rest in their graves.

Life should be a dance. And everybody's life can be a dance. It should be a music—and then you can share; you will have to share.

I don't have to say it, because this is one of the fundamental laws of existence: the more you share your bliss, the more it grows.

But I teach selfishness.

DON'T BE A LAWYER, BE A LOVER

In Matthew 22 is it said:

> Then one of them, which was a lawyer, asked him a question, tempting him, and saying, Master, which is the great commandment in the law?
>
> Jesus said unto him, thou shalt love the Lord thy God with all thy heart, and with all thy soul, and with all thy mind. This is the first and great commandment. And the second is like unto it, thou shalt love thy neighbor as thyself.
>
> On these two commandments hang all the law and the prophets.

Two words—law and love—are tremendously significant. They represent two types of mind, the polar opposites. The mind that is legal can never be loving, and the mind that loves can never be legal. The legal attitude is irreligious; it is political, social. And the attitude of love is non-political, non-social—individual, personal, religious.

Moses, Manu, Marx, Mao, these are the legal minds; they have given the law to the world. Jesus, Krishna, Buddha, Lao Tzu, these are the people of love. They have not given a legal commandment to the world, they have given a totally different vision.

I have heard a story about Frederick the Great, the King of Prussia—he was a legal mind. A woman came to him and complained about her husband. She said, "Your Majesty, my husband treats me very badly."

Frederick the Great said, "That is not my business."

But the woman persisted. She said, "Not only that, Your Majesty, he speaks ill of you also."

Frederick the Great said, "That is none of your business." This is the legal mind.

The legal mind is always thinking of law, never of love. The legal mind thinks of justice but never of compassion; and justice that is without compassion can never be just. A justice which has no compassion in it is bound to be unjust; and a compassion that may appear unjust cannot be unjust. The very nature of compassion is to be just; justice follows compassion as a shadow. But compassion doesn't follow justice as a shadow, because compassion is the real thing, love is the real thing. Your shadow follows you; you don't follow your shadow. The shadow cannot lead, the shadow has to follow. And this is one of the greatest controversies of human history—whether God is love or law; whether God is just or compassionate.

The legal mind says God is law, is just. But the legal mind cannot know what God is, because God is just another name for love. The legal mind cannot reach to that dimension. The legal mind always goes on throwing responsibility on somebody else—the society, the economic structure, history. For the legal mind, the other is always responsible. Love takes the responsibility itself: it is always I who am responsible, not you.

Once you understand that you are responsible, you start blossoming. Law is an excuse. It is a cunningness of the mind, so that you can always protect yourself, defend yourself. Love is vulnerable, law is a defensive arrangement. When you love somebody, you don't talk law. When you love, law disappears—because love is the ultimate law. It needs no other law, it is enough unto itself. And when love protects you, you don't need any other protection. Don't be legalistic, otherwise you will miss all that is beautiful in life. Don't be a lawyer, be a lover; otherwise you will go on protecting yourself, and in the end you will find that there is nothing to protect—you have been protecting just an empty ego. And you can always find ways and means to protect the empty ego.

I have heard a story about Oscar Wilde. His first play was staged and it failed completely; it was a flop. When he came out of the theater hall, friends asked, "How did it go?" He said, "It was a great success. But the audience was a great failure."

This is the legal mind, always trying to protect the empty ego—nothing but a soap bubble, hollow within, full of emptiness and nothing in it. But the law goes on protecting it. Remember, the moment you become legalistic, the moment you start looking at life through the law—maybe the law is that of the government, or the law is that of the church, it makes no difference—the moment you start looking at life through the law, through the moral code, the scripture, the commandment, you start missing it.

One needs to be vulnerable to know what life is; one needs to be totally open, insecure. One needs to be able to die in knowing it—only then one comes to know life. If you are afraid of death you will never know

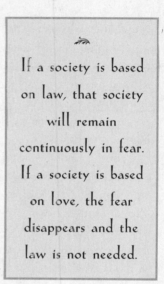

If a society is based on law, that society will remain continuously in fear. If a society is based on love, the fear disappears and the law is not needed.

life, because fear can never know. If you are unafraid of death, if you are ready to die to know it, you will know life, eternal life, which never dies. Law is hidden fear, love is expressed fearlessness.

When you love, fear disappears—have you observed? When you love, there is no fear. If you love a person, fear disappears. The more you love, the more fear disappears. If you love totally, fear is absolutely absent. Fear arises only when you don't love. Fear is an absence of love, law is an absence of love, because law is basically nothing but a defense of your inner, trembling heart—you are afraid, you want to protect yourself.

If a society is based on law, that society will remain continuously in fear. If a society is based on love, the fear disappears and the law is not needed—courts will not be needed; hell and heaven will not be needed. Hell is a legal attitude; all punishment comes from the legal mind. The law says if you do wrong you will be punished; if you do right you will be rewarded. And then there are so-called religions—they say if you commit sin you will be thrown into hell. Just think about their hell! These people who have created the idea of hell must have been very deeply sadistic. The way they have depicted hell, they have made every arrangement possible to make you suffer. And they have invented heaven also—heaven for themselves and for those who follow them, hell for those who don't follow them and don't believe in them. But these are legalistic attitudes, the same attitude as criminal punishment. And punishment has failed.

Crime cannot be stopped, it has not been stopped by punishment. It goes on growing, because in fact the legal mind and the criminal mind are two sides of the same coin; they are not different. All legal minds are basically criminal, and all criminal minds can become good legal minds—they have the potential. They are not two separate worlds; they are part of one world. Crime goes on increasing, and the law goes on becoming more and more complicated and complex.

Man has not been changed by punishment; in fact, he has been more corrupted. Courts have not changed him; they have corrupted him more. And neither have the concepts of reward, heaven, respectability, been of any help. Because hell depends on fear, and heaven depends on greed—fear and greed, those are the problems. How can you change people through them? They are the diseases, and the legal mind goes on saying they are the medicines.

A totally different attitude is needed, the attitude of love. Christ brings love to the world. He destroys law, the very basis of it. That was his crime; that's why he was crucified—because he was destroying the whole basis of this criminal society; he was destroying the whole foundation stone of this criminal world, the world of wars, and violence, and aggression. He gave a totally new foundation stone. These few lines have to be understood as deeply as possible.

Then one of them, which was a lawyer, asked him a question, tempting him, and saying . . .

"Tempting him" . . . He wanted to pull Jesus down into a legal argument. There are many instances in Jesus's life where he was tempted to come down from the heights of love to the dark valleys of law. And the people who tried to tempt him were very tricky. Their questions were such that if Jesus were not really a realized one, he would have fallen victim. They gave him what is called in logic "dilemmas"—whatever you answer, you will be caught. If you say this, you will be caught; if you say the opposite, then you will also be caught.

You must have heard the famous story. He is sitting by the side of the river; the crowd has come, and they have brought a woman. They say to him that this woman has committed sin: "What do you say?" They tempted him; because it is said in the old scriptures that if a woman commits sin, she should be stoned to death. Now they are giving two alternatives to Jesus. If he says follow the scripture, then they will ask, "Where has your concept of love and compassion gone? Can't you forgive her? So all that talk of love is just talk?" Then he will be caught. Or, if he says, "Forgive her," then they will say, "Then you are against the scripture; and you have been saying to people, 'I have come to fulfill the scripture, not to destroy it.'" This is a dilemma; now these are the only two alternatives.

But the legal mind is not aware that a man of love has a third alternative, which the legal mind cannot know about because the legal mind can only think in opposites. Only two alternatives exist for the legal mind, yes or no. It does not know about the third alternative, which de Bono has called *po*—yes, no, and the third alternative is *po*. It is neither yes nor no; it is totally different. Jesus is the first man in the world to say *po*. He didn't use the term, the term has been invented by de Bono—but he said *po*, he actually did it. He said to these people in the crowd, "Only those people amongst you who have never sinned, and never thought of committing sins, you should come forward. You should take stones in your hands and kill this woman." Now there was not a single one who had not committed sin, or who had not thought of committing it.

There may be people who have not committed sin, but they may be thinking continuously about it. In fact, they are bound to think about it. People who commit sin think less about it. Those who don't, continually think and fantasize about it. And for the innermost core of your being, it makes no difference whether you think or you act.

By and by the crowd started disappearing. People who were standing in front disappeared to the back—the legal experts of the society, the prominent citizens of the town started disappearing. This man had used a third alternative. He didn't say yes, he didn't say no. He said, "Yes, kill the woman—but only those who have never committed sin nor thought about it should kill her." The crowd disappeared. Jesus was left alone with the woman; she fell at his feet and said, "I have really committed sin, I am a bad woman. You can punish me."

Jesus said, "Who am I to judge? This is between you and your God. This is something between you and existence. Who am I to interfere? If you realize that you have done something wrong, don't do it again."

Such situations were continually repeated. The whole effort of people was to bring Jesus into an argument where the legal mind could succeed. You cannot argue with the legal mind—if you argue you will be defeated because in argument the legal mind is very efficient. Whatever position you take matters not; you will be defeated.

Jesus could not be defeated because he never argued. This is one of the signs, one of the indications that he had attained to love. He remained on his peak; he never descended.

Then one of them, which was a lawyer, asked him a question, tempting him, and saying, Master, which is the great commandment in the law?

Now, it is a very difficult question. Which is the great commandment, which is the foremost commandment, which is the fundamental commandment in law? It is very difficult, because every law depends on other laws—they are interlinked. You cannot find the basic law, because no law is basic. They depend on each other; they are interdependent.

In India it has been one of the ongoing debates: Which is basic—non-violence or truth? If you are in a situation where you have to choose between truth or non-violence—if you say the truth, then there will be violence, and if you don't say the truth, the violence can be avoided—what will you do? Will you say the truth and help the violence to be committed?

For example, you are standing at a crossroads, and a group of policemen come. They ask you, "Have you seen a man pass this way? He has to be caught and killed, he has escaped from prison. He is sentenced to death." You have seen the man. You can say yes and speak truthfully, but then you will be responsible for the death of that man. You can say you have not seen him, or you can even give the police wrong directions; then that man will be saved. You remained nonviolent, but you became untrue. What will you do? It seems impossible to choose, almost impossible. Which law is the most fundamental?

Jesus said unto him, thou shall love the Lord thy God with all thy heart, and with all thy soul, and with all thy mind.

This is *po*: he is not answering the question at all; he is answering something else. He is not getting down to the legal world; he remains perched on his peak of love. He says, "This is the first and great commandment: Love thy God with all thy heart, all thy mind, and all thy soul." The question was about law, and the answer is about love. In fact, he has not answered the question; or, you can say he has answered the question because this is the *only* answer, there can be no other answer.

This has to be understood. Only from a higher plane can the question of a lower plane be answered; remaining on the same plane, the answer is impossible. For example, from where you are the question arises, many questions arise. If you ask a person who remains on the same plane as you, he cannot answer you. His answers may look relevant, but cannot be relevant, because he is also in the same situation as you.

It is like a madman helping another madman, the blind leading the blind, a confused man helping another confused man to attain to clarity. More muddledness, more confusion will happen out of it. That's what has happened in the world—everybody is advising everybody else. Nothing is cheaper than advice. In fact, it costs nothing, you can have it just for the asking; everybody is ready to give you advice. Neither do you think about it, nor do those who are giving you advice, about the fact that they exist on the same plane, and their advice is simply useless. Or, it can be even harmful. Only somebody who is on a higher plane than you can be of any help—one who has a clearer perception, a deeper clarity, a more crystallized being. Only that type of person can answer your questions.

There are three possibilities of dialogue: one is two ignorant persons talking. Much talking goes on, but nothing happens out of it; it is just bogus. They talk, but they don't mean what they are saying, they are not even aware of what they are saying—it is just an occupation; it feels good to be occupied. They are talking like mechanical things, two computers talking. Then there is the possibility of two enlightened persons talking. They don't talk; there is no need to talk. The communion is silent; they understand each other without the words. Two ignorant persons talking—too many words, and no understanding. Two enlightened persons meeting—no words, only understanding. The first situation happens every day, millions of times all over the earth. The second situation happens rarely, after thousands and thousands of years—rarely does it happen that two enlightened persons meet.

There is a third possibility—one <u>enlightened person talking</u> to an <u>unenlightened person</u>. Then there are two planes: one is on the earth, the other is in the sky; one is moving in a bullock cart, the other is flying in an airplane. The person on the earth asks one thing and the person in the sky answers something else. But this is the only way, this is the only way the person on the earth can be helped. The lawyer had asked about the law. He had asked, *Master, which is the great commandment in the law?*

He is not asking about love. Jesus is trying to seduce him towards love—he has changed the whole context. Once it is in Jesus's hands, then he will take you into a dimension you know not, into the unknown, into the unknowable.

Jesus said unto him, thou shalt love the Lord thy God with all thy heart, and with all thy soul, and with all thy mind.

"With all thy heart" means with all your feelings. That is what prayerfulness is. <u>When all your feelings are</u> together, integrated into one unity, it is <u>prayer. Prayerfulness is your total heart,</u> throbbing with the desire of the unknown, <u>throbbing with a deep urge, a deep inquiry</u> into the unknown, each beat of your heart devoted.

"With all thy mind"—that is the meaning of meditation, when all your thoughts have become one. When all your thoughts become one, thinking disappears; when all your feelings become one, feeling disappears. When your feelings are many, you are sentimental. When your

> When your feelings are many, you are sentimental. When your feelings are one, all sentimentality disappears—you are full of heart but without any sentimentality.

feelings are one, all sentimentality disappears—you are full of heart but without any sentimentality. Prayerfulness is not sentimentalism. Prayerfulness is such a harmony of feelings, such a total unity of feelings that the quality of the feelings immediately changes. Just as you put water on to heat, it goes on becoming warmer, warmer, hotter and hotter—up to ninety-nine degrees centigrade it is still water. Then the hundred-degree point comes, and suddenly there is a transformation. The water is no longer water, it starts evaporating—the quality immediately changes. Water has the quality to flow downwards: when it evaporates, the vapor has the quality to float upwards. The dimension has changed.

When you live in feelings, so many feelings, you are just a confusion, a madhouse. When all the feelings are integrated, there comes a moment of transformation. When they all become one, you are at the hundred-degree point, the evaporating point. Immediately the old nature of the feelings disappears, the old down-flowing quality is no longer there. You start evaporating like vapor towards the sky. That is what prayerfulness is.

And the same thing happens when all your thoughts are one—thinking stops. When thoughts are many, thinking is possible; when thoughts are one, then there comes a moment that this oneness of thought becomes almost synonymous with no-thought. To have one thought is to have no thought, because the one cannot exist alone. The one can exist only with the many, the one can exist only in a crowd. When the crowd has disappeared, the one also disappears, and there comes a state of no-thought.

So Jesus, in his small sentence, has condensed the whole of religion:

Thou shalt love the lord thy God with all thy heart—this is what prayer is all about. *With all thy mind*—that is what meditation is all about.

And with all thy soul . . . The soul is the transcendence of thinking and feeling. The soul is beyond prayer and beyond meditation.

The soul is your nature—it is the transcendental consciousness in you.

Look at yourself as a triangle—on the lower base, feeling, thinking. But feeling and thinking are the only two that you have been experiencing up to now; you don't know the third. The third can be known only when the feeling becomes prayerfulness and starts moving upwards, and thinking becomes meditation and starts moving upwards. Then prayer and meditation meet at a point—that point is soul. Somewhere your heart and your mind meet—that is you, that is a beyondness. That's what Jesus calls the soul.

This is the first and great commandment.

Now he is using the language of the lawyer. He has said whatever he wanted to say; now he comes to the language of the lawyer. The first sentence belongs to Jesus's plane; the second sentence belongs to the lawyer's plane. And Jesus has tried to create a bridge between the two.

This is the first and the great commandment. Love is the first and the great commandment. In fact, love is not a commandment at all, because you cannot be commanded to love; you cannot be ordered to love, you cannot be forced. You cannot manage and control love. Love is bigger than you, higher than you—how can you control it? And if you are commanded to love, if somebody comes just as they do in the army: "Right turn! Left turn!"—somebody comes and says, "Love!" what can you do? "Right turn" is okay, "Left turn" is okay, but "Love'?—you don't know where to turn, where to go. You don't know the way, it cannot be commanded.

Yes, you can pretend; you can act. That's what has happened on this earth. The greatest curse that has happened on this earth is that love has been forced. From the very childhood everybody is taught to love, as if love can be taught: "Love your mother, love your father, love your brothers and sisters." Love this, love that—and the child starts trying, because how can the child know that love cannot be an act? It is a happening. You cannot force it.

You have been missing love because you have been trying too hard. And everybody is in search of love—you may call it God, you may call it something else, but deep down you are in search of love. But you have become incapable—not because you have not tried, but because you have tried too hard.

Love is a happening; it cannot be commanded. Because you have been commanded to love, your love has been falsified from the very beginning, poisoned from the very source. Never say to a child—never commit this sin—never say to a child, "Love your mother." Love the child and let love happen. Don't say, "Love me because I am your mother, or I am your father. Love me." Don't make it a commandment; otherwise your child will miss forever and ever. Just love the child, and in a loving milieu, one day suddenly the chord just happens. The harmony is found in the innermost organ of your being. Something starts; some melody, some harmony arises, and then you know that it is your nature. But then you never try to do it; then you simply relax and allow it to be.

> Love the child and let love happen. Don't say, "Love me because I am your mother, or I am your father. Love me." Don't make it a commandment.

This is the first and great commandment. Jesus is using the language of the lawyer, because he is answering him; otherwise love is not a commandment, and cannot be a commandment.

And the second is like unto it, thou shalt love thy neighbor as thyself:

The first is, love thy God. "God" means the total, the Tao, the Brahma. God is not a very good word; Tao is far better—the total, the whole, existence—love existence. That is the first, the most fundamental.

And the second is like unto it, thou shalt love thy neighbor as thyself:

. . . because it is difficult to find God, and it is difficult to love God if you have not found him already. How can you love God, who is unknown? How can you love the unknown? You need some bridge, you need some familiarity—how can you love God? It looks absurd, it *is* absurd. Hence the second commandment.

And the second is like unto it, thou shalt love thy neighbor as thyself:

I was reading a story—I liked it. A learned man asked Rabbi Abraham, "They say that you give people mysterious drugs, and that your drugs are effective. Give me one, that I may attain to the fear of God."

"I don't know any drug for the fear of God," said the Rabbi. "But, if you like, I can give you one for the love of God."

"That is even better!" cried the scholar. "Just give it to me."

"It is the love of one's fellow men," answered the Rabbi.

If you really want to love God, you have to start by loving your fellow human beings, because they are the nearest to you. And by and by, ripples of your love can go on expanding. Love is like a pebble thrown into a silent lake: ripples arise, and then they start spreading to the faraway shores. But first there is the touch of the pebble on the lake; close to the pebble the ripples arise, and then far and far away they spread. First, you will have to love those who are like you—because you know them, because at least you can feel a certain familiarity, a certain at-homeness with them. Then the love can go on expanding. Then you can love animals, then you can love trees, then you can love rocks. And then only can you love existence as such, not before then.

So, if you can love human beings, you have taken the first step. But just the opposite has been happening on this unfortunate earth—people love God and kill human beings. In fact, they say because they love God so much, they have to kill. Christians kill Mohammedans, Mohammedans kill Christians, Hindus kill Mohammedans, Mohammedans kill Hindus, because they all love God—in the name of

God, they kill human beings. Their gods are false. Because if your god is true, if you have really known what godliness means, if you have realized even a bit, if you have even attained just a glimpse of what godliness is, you will love human beings. You will love animals, you will love trees, you will love rocks—you will love! Love will become your natural state of being. And if you cannot love human beings, don't be deceived—no temple is going to help you.

You can say no to God, but never say no to human beings, because if you say no to human beings the path is cut; then you will never be able to reach godliness. Say no to the church, to the temple; there is no problem about it. But never say no to love, because that is the real temple. All other temples are just false coins, false images, not authentic. There is only one authentic temple, and that temple is love. Never say no to love—you will find godliness; it cannot hide for long.

The second commandment, Jesus says, *Thou shalt love thy neighbor as thyself* . . . because, in fact, all humanity is you, in many faces and in many forms. Can't you see it—that your neighbor is nobody other than you, your own being in a different shape and form?

Many rivers in the world are named after colors. In China we have the Yellow River; somewhere in South Africa they have the Red River. In the U.S., I have heard, they have the White River, the Green River. A river itself has no color; water is colorless, but the river takes the colors of the terrain it passes through, the color of the shrubbery on the banks. If it passes a desert, of course it has a different color; if it passes through a forest, the forest is reflected—the shrubbery, the greenery—it has a different color. If it passes through a terrain where the mud is yellow, it becomes yellow. But no river has any color. And every river, whether it is called white, or green, or yellow, reaches naturally to its end, to its destiny, falls into the ocean, and becomes oceanic.

Your differences are because of your terrain. Your colors are different because of your terrain. But your innermost quality of being is colorless; it is the same. Somebody is black, somebody is white;

somebody is just in the middle, an Indian; somebody is yellow, a Chinese—so many colors. But remember, these are the colors of the terrain of the body you pass through. They are not your colors; you are colorless. You are not the body; neither are you the mind, nor are you the heart. Your mind differs, because it has been conditioned differently; your body is different, because it has come through a different terrain, through a different heredity; but you are not different.

Jesus says: Thou shalt love thy neighbor as thyself. As you love yourself, love your neighbor. And one thing very basic, which Christians have completely forgotten. Jesus says—"Love thyself." Unless you love yourself, you cannot love your neighbor. All the so-called Christianity has been teaching you is hatred towards yourself, condemnation of yourself. Love yourself, because you are the nearest to godliness. It is there that the first ripple has to arise. Love yourself! Self-love is the most fundamental thing—if you ever want to be religious, self-love is the basis. And all so-called religions go on teaching you self-hatred: "Condemn yourself, you are a sinner, guilty, this and that—you are worthless."

You are not a sinner. They have made you so. You are not guilty; they have given you wrong interpretations of life. Accept yourself, and love yourself. Only then can you love your neighbor, otherwise there is no possi-

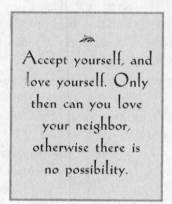

Accept yourself, and love yourself. Only then can you love your neighbor, otherwise there is no possibility.

bility. If you don't love yourself, how can you love another being? I teach you self-love. At least do that; if you cannot do anything else—love yourself. And out of your self-love, by and by you will see that love is starting to flow; it is expanding; it is reaching to the neighbors.

The whole problem today is that you hate yourself and you want to love somebody else, which is impossible. And the other also hates himself, and he wants to love you. The lesson of love has to be learned first within yourself.

If you ask Freud and the psychoanalysts, they have come to discover a very basic thing. They say that first the child is autoerotic, masturbatory; the child loves himself. Then the child becomes homosexual—the boys love boys and want to play with boys; girls want to play with girls, and they don't want to mix with each other. And then arises heterosexuality—the boy wants to mix and love a girl; a girl wants to meet a boy and love. First, autoerotic, then homoerotic, then heteroerotic—this is about sex. The same is true about love.

First, you love yourself. Then you love your neighbor, you love other human beings. And then you move beyond and you love existence. But the basis is you. So don't condemn yourself; don't reject yourself. Accept. The divine has taken abode in you. Existence has loved you so much, that's why it has taken abode in you. Existence has made a temple of you; the divine lives in you. If you reject yourself, you reject the nearest to godliness that you can find. If you reject the nearest, it is impossible that you will be able to love the faraway.

When Jesus says, "Thou shalt love thy neighbor as thyself," he is saying two things: First, love thyself, so that you can be capable of loving thy neighbor.

On these two commandments hang all the law and the prophets.

In fact it is one commandment: Love. Love is the one and only order of things. If you have understood love, you have understood all. If you have not understood love, you may know many things but all that knowledge is simply rot. Throw it on a rubbish heap and forget all about it. Start from the very beginning. Be a child again, and start loving yourself again.

Your lake, as I see it, has no ripples. The first pebble of love has not fallen in it.

I have heard a Danish story. Remember it, let it become part of your mindfulness. The story tells about a spider who lived high up in the rafters of an old barn. One day he let himself down by a long thread to a lower beam, where he found the flies were more plentiful and more easily caught. He decided to live permanently at this lower level, and spun himself a comfortable web there. But one day he happened to notice the line down which he had come, stretching away into the darkness above. "I don't need this anymore," he said. "It only gets in the way." He snapped it, and with it destroyed his whole web, which needed it for support.

This is the story of man also. A thread joins you with the ultimate, the highest—call it Tao, existence, godliness. You may have completely forgotten that you descended from there. You come from the whole, and you have to go back to it. Everything goes back to the original source; it has to be so. Then the circle is complete and one is fulfilled. And you may even feel like this spider, that the thread that joins you to the highest comes in the way. Many times because of it you cannot do some things; again and again it comes in the way. You cannot be violent as you would like to be; you cannot be aggressive as you would like to be; you cannot hate as much as you would like to hate—the line again and again comes in the way. Sometimes you may feel like this spider—to cut it, to snip at it so that your path is clear.

That's what Nietzsche says: "God is dead." He snapped the line. But immediately Nietzsche went mad. The moment he said "God is dead" he went mad, because then you are cut away from the original source of all life. Then you are starved of something vital, essential. Then you miss something, and you had become completely oblivious that it was the very base of your life. The spider snapped the thread, and with it destroyed his whole web, which needed it for support.

Wherever you are, in your darkest night, a ray of light is still joined with you from existence. That is your life; that's how you are alive. Find that thread, because that is going to be the way back home.

On 5th June, 1910, O. Henry was dying. It was getting dark. Friends were surrounding him. Suddenly he opened his eyes and said, "Put the light up. I don't want to go home in darkness." The light was put up; he closed his eyes, smiled, and disappeared.

The thread that is joining you, the single ray of life that is making you alive, is the way back home. However far you have gone, you are still joined with existence—otherwise it would not be possible. You may have forgotten, but existence has not forgotten you; and that is the real thing that matters. Try to find something in you which joins you to existence. Search for it, and you will come to the commandment that Jesus is talking about. If you search, you will come to know it is love, not knowledge, that joins you to existence. Not riches, not power, not fame—it is love that joins you to existence. And whenever you feel love, you are tremendously happy because more and more life becomes available to you.

Jesus, or Buddha, both are like honeybees. The honeybee goes and finds beautiful flowers in a valley. She comes back, she dances a dance of ecstasy near her friends to tell them that she has found a beautiful valley full of flowers. "Come, follow me." A Jesus is just a honeybee who has found the original source of life—a valley of beautiful flowers, flowers of eternity. He comes and dances near you to give you the message: "Come, follow me."

If you try to understand and seek within, you will find it is love that is the most significant, most essential thing in your being. Don't starve it. Help it to grow, so that it can become a big tree; so that birds of heaven can take shelter in you; so that in your love, tired travelers on the path can rest; so that you can share your love; so that you can also become a honeybee. In your ecstasy, you can also share with people what you have found.

CRIME AND PUNISHMENT

The death penalty is degrading proof of man's inhumanity to man. It shows that man is still living in the barbarous age. Civilization still remains an idea—it has not become a reality.

You will have to look from all the aspects to understand why such an idiotic thing as the death penalty has continued to be used in so many civilizations, cultures, nations. Even in some countries where it was dropped it has been adopted again. In other countries where it has been dropped, it has been replaced by life imprisonment—which is worse than the death penalty itself. It is better to die in a single moment than to go on dying slowly for fifty years, sixty years. Changing from the death penalty to a life sentence is going not towards civilization, it is going still deeper into barbarous, inhuman darkness, unconsciousness.

The first thing to understand is that the death penalty is not really a punishment. If you cannot give life as a reward, you cannot give death as a penalty. This is simple logic, there cannot be two opinions about it. If you cannot give life to people, what right have you to take their life?

I am reminded of a true story. It happened that two criminals found a treasure that was hidden in a castle. Many times people had tried to break into the castle and steal it, and had been caught, but somehow these criminals succeeded. The treasure was vast, and one of the two decided that he was not willing to divide it. One way was to kill the other, but in killing the other he might get caught. He could not take any risk, because now the whole treasure was in his hands.

He managed in a very cunning way. He disappeared and spread the rumor that he had been murdered, and he left evidence to make it appear that his friend was the murderer. The friend was caught with all the evidence: his revolver had two bullets missing, and his finger-prints were on the revolver. A handkerchief with his name embroidered on it had been left at the scene. . . . He could not prove his innocence; there was no way—everything went against him and he was given the death penalty. He knew he had not murdered his friend; he knew that this whole thing was a plot. His friend was not dead; it was just a trick to keep the whole treasure to himself.

But the man escaped from prison before he was executed. And twelve years later, when he heard that the first man—who had changed his identity and become a respected politician—had died, he came to the authorities. He told the court—it was the same judge—"I am the man who you sentenced to death twelve years ago, but I escaped. And I was absolutely innocent, but I had no proof."

In fact innocence has never any proof. Proofs are for the crime or against the crime, but innocence has no proof. He said, "Now the man you charged me with murdering twelve years ago has died—this is the very same man. So I cannot have murdered him twelve years ago." He said, "The only crime I have committed is escaping from jail, but can you call it a crime? When you punish an innocent man with death, who is the criminal—you or me?"

The story has many implications. The man asked, "If I was sentenced to death and I had not escaped and was executed, what would have been the case now? If it had come to be known that the man thought to be murdered was alive, would you be able to give me my life back? If you cannot give my life back, what right have you to take it away?"

It is said that the judge resigned, apologized to the man and said, "Perhaps I have committed many crimes in my life."

All over the world, the reality is that unless you are proved innocent, you are guilty. This goes against all humanitarian ideals, democracy, freedom, respect for individuality; it goes against all. The rule says that until you are proved guilty you are innocent—this is what is said in words—but in reality the case is just the opposite.

Man goes on saying one thing and goes on doing just its opposite. He talks about being civilized, cultured—he is not civilized, not cultured. The death penalty is proof enough.

This is the rule of a barbarous society: an eye for an eye, and a head for a head. If somebody cuts off one of your hands, then in a barbarous society, it is a simple law that one of his hands should be cut off. The same has been carried down the ages and the death penalty is exactly the same law: "An eye for an eye. If a man is thought to have murdered somebody, then he should be murdered." But it is strange: if killing somebody is a crime, then how can you remove crime from society by committing the same crime again? There was one man murdered; now there are two men murdered. And it is not absolutely certain that this man murdered that man, because to prove a murder is not an easy thing.

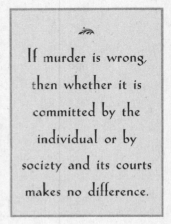

If murder is wrong, then whether it is committed by the individual or by society and its courts makes no difference.

If murder is wrong, then whether it is committed by the individual or by society and its courts makes no difference.

Killing certainly is a crime. The death penalty is a crime committed by the society against a single individual, who is helpless. I cannot call it a penalty, it is a crime.

And you can understand why it is committed: <u>it is a way of taking revenge.</u> Society is taking revenge because the person did not follow the rules. The society is ready to kill him—but nobody bothers that when somebody commits a murder it shows that person is psychologically sick. Rather than sending him to prison or to be executed, he should be sent into a facility where he can be taken care of—physically, psychologically, spiritually. He is sick; he needs all the compassion of the society, there is no question of punishment.

Yes, it is true—one man is murdered. But we cannot do anything about it. By murdering the person who killed the man do you think the other will come back to life? If that were possible, I would be all in support of this murderer being removed—he is not worth being part of the society—and the other should be revived. But that does not happen. The other is gone forever; there is no way to revive him. Yes, you can do one thing, you can kill this man too. You are trying to wash away blood with blood, mud with mud.

You are not aware of what has happened in history in many cases. Three hundred years ago, in many cultures the madman was thought to be pretending. In many other cultures he was thought to be possessed by ghosts. In other cultures he was thought to be mad, but treatable by punishment. These were the three ways mad people were taken care of.

They were treated with beatings—strange treatment!—and by taking their blood out. Now you give blood transfusions; they used to do just the opposite—they used to take the blood out of the person because it was thought that he had too much energy. Naturally, when blood was taken out the person became weak, started showing signs of weakness because so much blood was taken out, and it was thought they had cured him of his madness.

By beating people, naturally once in a while it used to happen that they came to their senses. It is almost as if a person is asleep and you start beating him and he wakes up. A madman has fallen out of his conscious mind; if you beat him hard, once in a while it may happen that he wakes up into his consciousness again. That became proof that the beating was the right treatment. It used to happen only once in a while; ninety-nine percent of the cases were unnecessarily tortured. But that one exception became the rule.

It was thought that mad people were possessed by spirits, ghosts; then too the idea was to beat them, because if they were possessed by ghosts, the beating would only affect the ghost, not the person. You are not beating the person's body, you are really beating the ghosts who are possessing the person, and because of the beating the ghosts will escape. And once in a while the person would come to his senses—but just once in a while, less than one percent, no more than that.

I have been in one place that was famous for treating mad people. Hundreds of mad people were brought to that place. It was a temple on the bank of a river, and the priest of that temple must have been a butcher for at least a few hundred lives. He looked like a butcher and he gave everybody a good beating. Those mad people were chained, given a good beating, no food, and very strong laxatives. And I have seen that once in a while a person came to his senses. Strong laxatives for a few days with no food cleaned his inner system. Beatings brought him back a little consciousness. No food, hunger—a hungry man cannot afford to be mad because his body is in such torture. To be mad you need a little bit of comfort in your life situation.

You can see it—the more comfortable a society, the more luxurious, affluent a culture, the more people go mad. The poorer a society—starving, hungry—the less people go mad. Madness needs, in the first place, a mind. But a hungry person has no nourishment for the mind. He is undernourished, so his mind is not in a situation to go nuts. For that the mind needs more energy than ordinarily is involved in survival. Madness is a rich man's disease. The poor cannot afford it.

So when you keep a person hungry and give him laxatives, it cleanses his inner system, makes him so hungry that he becomes bodily oriented. He forgets the mind, the primary concern is the body. He is no longer interested in the mind and its mind games.

Madness is a mind game.

So once in a while I saw people being cured in that temple, but that one percent who were cured would cause the rumor to spread all around, and hundreds of people were taken there. The temple became very rich. I had gone there many times to see it, but only once did I meet a man who had been cured; others went back to their homes just beaten, hungry, starved—even more sick, more weak. Many died because of that priest's treatment.

But in India, if the treatment is being given by a priest in a temple, a sacred place, it is not a crime if you die; in fact you are thought to be fortunate that you have died in a sacred place. You will be reborn on a higher level of consciousness. So it is not considered to be a crime. And priests have been treating mad people for centuries, in the same way, all over the world.

Now we know that a mad person cannot be treated in this way. Mad people were put into prison, into isolated cells. That is still happening around the world because we don't know what else to do. Just to hide our ignorance we put the mad people into jail, so we can forget about them; at least we can go on ignoring the fact that they exist.

In my town one of my friends' uncles was mad. They were rich people. I used to go to their house often, but even I became aware only after years that one of this friend's uncles was kept in an underground basement, chained.

I asked, "Why?"

They said, "He is mad. There were only two ways: either we keep him in our own house, chained. . . . And of course we cannot keep him chained upstairs in the house; otherwise people will be coming to visit, and everybody will feel worried and concerned. And his children, his wife, watching their father, their husband in this state . . . it would be terrible. It would damage our family's reputation to send him to prison, so we found a way. We have imprisoned him underground. His food is taken to him by a servant; otherwise nobody goes to see him, nobody goes to meet with him."

I persuaded my friend, "I would like to meet your uncle."

He said, "But I cannot come with you—he is a dangerous man, he is mad! Even though he is chained, he might do anything."

I said, "He can at the most kill me. You just remain behind me so if I am killed you can escape—but I would like to go."

Because I insisted, he managed to get the key from the servant who took care of the uncle's food. In thirty years I was the first person from the outside world, other than the servant, who had met him. And that man may have been mad at one time—I cannot say—but now he was not mad. But nobody was ready to listen to him because all mad people say, "We are not mad." So when he would say this to the servant, "Tell my family that I am not mad," the servant would simply laugh. Finally the servant even told the family, but nobody took any note of it.

When I saw the man I sat with him, I talked with him. He was as sane as anybody else in the world—perhaps a little more, because he said one thing to me: "Being here for thirty years has been a tremendous experience. In fact I feel fortunate that I am out of your mad world. They think I am mad—let them think it, there is no harm—but in fact I am fortunate that I am out of your mad world. What do you think?" he said to me.

I said, "You are absolutely right. The world outside is far madder than when you left it thirty years ago. In thirty years there has been great evolution in everything—in madness too. You should stop telling people that you are not mad; otherwise they might take you out! You are living a perfectly beautiful life. You have enough space to walk around. . . ."

> Mad people need methods of meditation so that they can come out of their madness. Criminals need psychological help, spiritual support. They are really deep-down sick, and you are punishing sick people.

He said, "That's the only exercise I can do here—walking."

I started to teach him vipassana. I said, "You are in such a perfect situation to become a buddha: no worries, no botherations, no disturbances. You are really blessed." And the last time I saw him, before he died, I could see from his face, from his eyes, that he was not the same person—a total transformation, a mutation had happened to him.

Mad people need methods of meditation so that they can come out of their madness. Criminals need psychological help, spiritual support. They are really deep-down sick, and you are punishing sick people. It is not their fault. If somebody murders, that means he has carried a tendency to murder in him for a long time. It is not that somewhere, out of nowhere, suddenly you murder somebody.

If a murder happens then the society needs to be looked at, then the whole society should have to pay the penalty. Why did such a thing happen in this society? What have you done with the man that he had to commit a murder? Why did he become destructive?—because nature gives everybody energy that is creative. It becomes destructive only when it is obstructed, when no natural flow is allowed. Whenever energy goes towards the natural it is prevented by society, it is crippled; it is diverted into some other direction. Soon the man is in a confusion. He does not know what is what. He does not know what he is doing, why he is doing it. The original reasons are left far behind; he has taken so many turns that he has become a jigsaw puzzle.

Nobody needs the death penalty, nobody deserves it. In fact, not just the death penalty, no other kind of punishment is right either, because punishment never cures the person. Every day the number of criminals goes on growing; every day you build more prisons. This is strange. It should not be so. Just the opposite should be the case, because with so many courts and so many punishments and so many prisons, crime should be less, criminals should be fewer. Over time, the prisons should be fewer, courts should be fewer. And that is not happening.

It is because your whole reasoning is wrong. You cannot teach by punishing people. That's what your jurists, legal experts, politicians, have been saying down the ages: "If we don't punish people, then how are we going to teach them? Then everybody will start committing crime. We have to go on punishing people so they remain afraid." They think fear is the only way to teach—and fear is not the way to teach people at all! What punishment does is to teach people to be acquainted with fear, so the original shock is no longer there. They know what can happen: "At the most you can beat me. And if one person can take it, I can also take it. Besides, out of a hundred thieves you can catch only one or two persons. Now, if you are not ready even to take that much risk—ninety-eight percent success, two percent failure—what kind of man are you?"

Nobody learns from punishment. Even the person who is being punished does not learn what you want him to learn. Yes, he learns something else; he learns to have a thick skin.

And once a person goes into prison, prison becomes his home because there he finds people of a like mind. There he finds his real society. Outside he was a foreigner; in prison he is in his own world. They all understand the same language, and there are experts. You may be just an amateur, an apprentice; it may be your first term.

I have heard a story about one man who enters a prison, and in the dark cell he sees an old man, resting. The old man asks him, "For how long are you going to be here?"

The newcomer says, "For ten years."

The old man says, "Then you can stay close to the door. Only ten years! You seem to be an amateur. I am going to be here for fifty years, so you just stay close to the door. Soon you will be out."

But when you are with experts for ten years, of course you learn all their techniques, strategies, methods. You learn from their experience. You will find your jails to be a kind of university where crime is taught at government expense. You will find professors of crime, deans of the crime faculty, vice-chancellors, chancellors—all kinds of people who have committed every kind of crime that you can imagine. Certainly the newcomer starts learning.

I have been to many prisons, and in all of them the climate was essentially the same. The common idea in all those jails and prisons I have visited is that it is not crime that brings you to jail, it is being caught. So you have to learn the right ways to do wrong things. It is not a question of doing right; the question is doing wrong in a right way. And every prisoner learns the right way of doing wrong things in jail. In fact I have talked with prisoners who have said, "We are eager to get out as soon as possible because we have learned so much, we want to practice. Just the practical aspects were missing, before we got caught it was all theoretical knowledge. For the practical teaching you need the society of the prison to teach you."

Once a person becomes a jailbird, then nowhere else will he find himself so at ease; sooner or later he will be coming back to jail. Over time, jail becomes his alternative society. It is more comfortable, he feels more at home; nobody looks down on him. Everybody is a criminal. Nobody is a priest and nobody is a sage and nobody is a holy man. All are poor human beings with all the weaknesses and frailties.

Outside he finds that he is rejected, abandoned.

In my town there was a permanent jailbird. He was a very beautiful man; his name was Barkat Mian and he would spend almost nine months in jail, then three months outside. In those three months he had to go to report to the police station every week to show that everything was okay and he was still here. But I had a great friendship with the man. My family was very angry; they said, "Why do you keep company with Barkat?" They used to say to me, "A man is known by his company."

I said, "I understand you. That means Barkat will be known by me, and to give a person a little respectability is not anything bad."

They said, "When will you see things in the right way?"

I said, "I am seeing it exactly the right way. Rather than Barkat degrading me, I am upgrading Barkat. You think his evil is more powerful than my goodness? You don't trust my integrity; you trust

Barkat's integrity." I said, "Whatever your opinion, I trust myself. Barkat cannot do any harm to me. If any harm is going to be done it will be done to Barkat by me."

He was really a beautiful man, nice, and he used to tell me, "You should not be around me. If you want to meet me and talk, we can manage to meet somewhere outside the town, by the riverbank." He himself lived near the Mohammedan cemetery where nobody goes unless one dies; one goes only once. He was not allowed to live in the town. In the town nobody was ready to give him a house to rent. No matter how much rent he was ready to pay, nobody would take it. Nobody was going to take him in.

I asked Barkat, "How did you become a thief?"

He said, "The first time I was jailed I was absolutely innocent, but I was poor and I could not hire a lawyer and the people who wanted me to be forced into jail had some vested interest. My father and mother died when I was very young, fourteen or fifteen. And my other relatives wanted to capture the whole family's possessions, the house, the land—but to do that they had to move me out of the way. They simply managed it. They put something into my bag in my house, and there was no way to get out of it. The thing was found in my bag, and I was sent to jail. When I came back, my land was gone, my house was sold, my relatives had managed to disperse and distribute everything. I was just on the streets.

"So, first, I was innocent when I went in, but when I came out I was not innocent, because I had graduated. I told everybody in jail what had happened to me—I was only seventeen—and they said 'Don't be worried, these nine months will be soon finished, but in nine months we will also give you the finishing touches and you will be able to take revenge on everybody.'

"First I started to take revenge on all the relatives—this was simply tit for tat. They had forced me to become a thief, and I proved that now I was a thief. I went after this whole gang of my relatives and stole everything they had. But by and by I became more and more involved. You can have ten cases in which you are saved, but in the eleventh you are caught. As you grow older and more efficient, you are caught less. But now there is no problem; in fact the prison is a relaxing place, a holiday from work and worry and all kinds of things. A few months in jail are good for the health—it is a disciplined life with an exact time to get up, to go to work, to go to sleep. And enough food to keep you alive."

He said, "I am never sick in jail, unless I pretend so that I can go to the hospital to have a little holiday. Outside I fall sick, but never inside. And outside is a foreign world; everybody is superior and I am inferior. Only in jail do I feel a sense of freedom."

Strange! When he said that, I said, "You say in jail you feel free?"

He said, "Yes, only in jail do I feel free."

> The world population has to be cut to one third if you want crime to disappear.

What kind of society is this, where people in jail feel free, and outside they feel imprisoned?

And this is almost the story of every criminal. A small thing in the beginning—maybe he was hungry, maybe he was cold, needed a blanket and just stole a blanket—small necessities that should be fulfilled; otherwise the society should not have produced these people. Nobody asks the society to produce them. On the one hand you go on producing people more and more, and there are not enough things for them, neither food nor clothes nor shelter. Then what do you expect? You are putting people in a situation where they are bound to become criminals.

The world population has to be cut to one third if you want crime to disappear.

But nobody wants crime to disappear because the disappearance of crime means the disappearance of your judges, of your lawyers, your legal experts, of your parliaments, your policemen, your jailers. It will create a big unemployment problem; nobody wants anything to change for the better.

Everybody says things should change for the better, but everybody goes on making things worse, because the worse things are the more people are employed. The worse things are the more chances you have to feel good. Criminals are needed for you to feel that you are such moral, respectable people. Sinners are needed for saints to feel that they are saints. Without sinners, who will be a saint? If the whole society consisted of good people, do you think you will remember Jesus Christ for two thousand years? For what? It is the criminal society that remembers Jesus Christ for two thousand years.

It is a simple thing to understand. Why do you remember Gautam Buddha? If there were millions of buddhas, awakened people, in the world you would not take any note. What specialty did Gautam Buddha have? He would have been lost in the crowd. But twenty-five centuries have passed and he stands like a pillar, a mountain peak far above your heads.

In fact Buddha, Jesus, Mohammed, Mahavira, are not giants—you are pygmies. And every giant has an investment in your remaining a pygmy; otherwise he won't be a giant. This is a great conspiracy.

I am against this whole conspiracy. I am neither a giant nor a pygmy. I have no vested interest at all. I am just myself. I don't compare myself with anybody, so nobody is lower than me and nobody is higher than me. Because of this simple fact I can see directly; there is no vested interest creating diversions to my vision. And this is my immediate response to the question of the death penalty—it is simply proof that man still needs to be civilized, needs to be cultured, needs to know human values.

In this world nobody is a criminal, never has been. Yes, there are people who need compassion—not imprisonment, not punishment. All prisons should be transformed into psychological nursing homes.

MATTERS OF LIFE AND DEATH–
RESPONSES TO QUESTIONS

My sister had an accident, and since then she can't move, she can't see, she can't hear, she can't speak. Is it better to let her die?

It is one of the most fundamental questions, which is being raised all around the earth in different forms. Because for centuries we have accepted the idea that death should be avoided, that it is something evil—that life is given by God, and death comes through the devil.

Even in the medical profession, every medical graduate in the world has to take the Hippocratic oath saying that he will not help anybody in any way to die; he will help in every possible way to protect life.

It was right in the days of Hippocrates, because out of every ten children born only one survived to become an adult. Nine were going to die, that was the situation. The entire world's population in the times of Gautam Buddha was so small you cannot imagine. It was only two hundred million. Now India alone has almost a billion people. The whole world has more than five billion people. From two hundred million people, in twenty-five centuries, we have reached more than five billion people, on the same Earth. And medical science has grown tremendously.

It used to be said that seventy years was the longest one could hope to live. For almost five thousand years, scientists have been searching for bones, skeletons, to find out exactly how long man used to live. And they have come to the conclusion that people were not living to more than forty years of age—so it is right when people say that in the past, the days were so beautiful that no father ever saw the death of his own son. It is natural. If every father is going to die at forty, how he is going to see the death of his own son?

But in this, those nine small children are not included, because they lived no more than two years. So in reality, every father was seeing dozens of his sons and daughters dying. Once a child had survived more than two years, then there was a possibility for him to live at least forty years. Naturally, meanwhile his father would be dying.

Now there are many people who have passed a hundred years of age and in some parts of the world you can find a man over a hundred years old who can still work in the field like any young man. Some scientists say that there is a possibility, if the right nutrition, the right exercise and right atmosphere is available, that a person's body is capable to live at least three hundred years. That is a very dangerous prospect, because even in ninety or a hundred years time, you get so fed up with life—what are you going to do for three hundred years? Your own family members will not recognize you. In three hundred years, so many generations of your own descendants—they will not have any relationship with you. The gap will be too great.

> If somebody for a whole month enjoys, is happy, is looking forward to death as an adventure, then it is our duty to allow these people to drop the body as gracefully as possible.

And what are you going to do? You have lived, you have loved. You have seen all that life contains—the failures, the successes; the pains and the pleasures, the days and the nights. You have seen all the seasons; now there is nothing more. It is now just repetition, the same wheel is moving.

We have to think again about the whole matter of death. My own opinion is that if a person comes to a stage where he finds that it is absolutely useless for him to live, he has lived enough, then it should not be illegal. It should be absolutely permissible; in fact, every hospital should have a special department for those people who come to die there—so they can die in peace, in silence, with all the appropriate medical care. This medical care is not to keep them alive, this medical care is to help them to die as beautifully, as silently as possible.

My own suggestion is that every death department in a hospital should have a meditator who can help people to learn meditation before they die, so they can die meditatively. Their death can become an immensely valuable experience, perhaps more valuable than their whole life has been. And they are not committing any sin.

You can have time to think about it. Perhaps the person is emotionally upset at the moment. Perhaps something has happened that has given them the idea, "It is better to finish my life." They should be given time, should be told, "You enter into the hospital, rest for one month, prepare for your death. We will help. But if during this one month you change your mind, it is up to you. You can get up and get out! Nobody is forcing you."

And remember, no emotion remains more than for a few minutes. Anybody who commits suicide, if he had waited a single minute more, may not have done it. It is a momentary thing. But if somebody for a whole month continuously enjoys, is happy, is really looking forward to death as an adventure, then it is our duty to allow these people to drop the body as gracefully as possible.

In response to the question, I had to give you this much introduction so that you can understand that death is not something evil, that it is something natural. But the question is not about an old person. The question is about a younger sister, who cannot move, who cannot see, who cannot hear, who cannot speak. All her senses are absent. Now, do you call it life? This is simply vegetation. And she must be in incredible suffering. That we cannot see, because she cannot say anything. She has no doors to communicate. She is absolutely alone, cut off from all life. What is the point of her vegetating for seventy, eighty or ninety years—or maybe more? She will be a burden on the family. She will be a source of sadness to the family and she herself will be in absolute hell, because she is completely imprisoned.

Just think of yourself. There cannot be a greater concentration camp: your eyes are taken away, your ears are closed, you cannot speak. You will be in a coma. There are many people in such situations. I myself have seen one woman, who was in coma for nine months. And the doctors were saying that she could never come back to consciousness because she had been unconscious for so long that the delicate nervous system that keeps one conscious had almost died. They showed me the scans of her brain, and they said that all the points that make one self-conscious had died. She would remain unconscious, and perhaps for fifty years, because she was not more than thirty when I saw her. Now she is a constant heaviness on the whole family, on the husband, on the children. They cannot do anything, they are simply helpless. The doctors cannot do anything, they are helpless. But the law prevents helping anybody to die, otherwise the doctors would be criminals. They would be thought to be murderers.

The law is primitive. The law does not understand compassion. That woman needs a merciful death. She cannot ask even for her death!

The questioner's sister cannot ask even for death. But those who love her should ask the government of whichever country they belong to. You should take her case to the court and insist that to keep her alive is not compassion. It is not love, it is an absolutely primitive idea, which has no contemporary support. Let them know that the whole family is ready, that she should be relieved from this prison so that she can get a new birth, a new body—with eyes, with ears, she can talk and she can walk. Her death will not be a calamity. Her death will be a blessing for her.

I am simply telling you my approach. I am not telling you to act accordingly, because that may be illegal in your county. You have to approach through the law to the government, and make it a point of national discussion, because it may not be only your sister. There may be many other children and young people suffering in the same

117

way—for no other reason except that the law does not permit any medical person to help somebody to drop the body.

It is time that we should understand, and the medical profession should understand—the Hippocratic oath should no longer be the oath for medical students. They should be given an oath that helps a person to live if he can live abundantly, more beautifully—but if the person cannot live and you simply go on helping him just to breathe . . . Breathing is not life. Then it is better to help the person to die. In both cases, you are compassionate. Either you serve life or you serve death—it does not matter. Your compassion should see that the person gets into a better space, into a better life.

And every country has to come to pass a law, just as the laws of most countries now accept birth control. That is one end of life; you are preventing children from being born. If you have accepted that, then on the other end you should allow old people who want to leave the world, to let them leave ceremoniously. They can call all their friends, their whole family. They can live with the whole family for one month, because now they are going to be here only for a month longer.

Birth is not in your hands, but at least you can be free to chose your death. A few more governments in the world are going to accept soon that on the other end of life also we should allow people to move faster. The world is too crowded. On one hand we are preventing people from coming, and on the other hand we should let them move on, so that the world becomes less crowded and less poor.

And it is not a question only of the world becoming less poor and less crowded, it is also a question of those people. In almost all of the western countries, and particularly in America, hundreds of thousands of people are simply living in hospitals. They are ninety years or a hundred years old. They cannot live in their homes, because they cannot even breathe on their own. And still we are keeping them alive—for what? Artificial breathing is being given to them. I don't think it is going to be a pleasure to those people. They will never be going back home. They will die in the hospital. And I don't see what is the logic of keeping them breathing artificially. When their bodies are not ready to breathe, please allow them not to breathe! That is their personal affair.

You are interfering too much. You won't let them die. They are already dead and you are forcing them to continue even though you are not aware of any purpose for it. And when you are keeping thousands of people alive who should be resting in their graves—unnecessarily occupying places in the hospitals, the time of the doctors, of so many machines and so much care—what is the purpose? After two or three years they will even stop taking the artificial breath in. They will refuse and reject it. Nothing else is going to happen. But for those three years you will be keeping them unnecessarily in torture. And this is thought to be service, this is thought to be compassion. This is thought to be Christian. This is simply cruelty!

Let those poor people die. And there are thousands of people around the world who are ready to leave the body because the body is only a pain to them. With so much disease, with so much sickness, they are no longer able to do anything. They are no longer able to enjoy anything.

But it is a very strange world. It goes on following old laws, which have lost all reality, which have become just shadows of the past and now they are torturing humanity unnecessarily.

My suggestion is that your sister should be released from this body, because this body is nothing but a prison to her. If you love her, you have to say good-bye to her. With tears, with sadness, but still you have to say good-bye to her and you have to meditate and pray that she gets into a better body. But ask the government, create a movement around it, so that not only your sister is helped. There may be many other people in her situation. And make as much uproar about it as you can, only then you will be allowed, so that your sister can have a peaceful death. And don't be worried—because your innermost being never dies.

The strongest thing in my Christian upbringing was to be unselfish, not to think of myself. Now, remembering myself and following the urge to turn inwards, I seem to have to push through a layer of unease, guilt and confusion. Would you speak about it?

> ⌒
>
> Unless you are selfish enough to know yourself, unselfishness is impossible. Unselfishness will come as a consequence of knowing yourself, of being yourself.

All the religions have done immense harm to man's growth, but Christianity is at the top as far as harming humanity is concerned. They have used beautiful words to hide ugly acts against you. For example, unselfishness—to tell a person who does not know himself or herself to be unselfish is so outrageously idiotic that one cannot believe Christianity has been doing it for two thousand years.

Socrates says, "Know thyself; anything else is secondary." Knowing yourself, you can be unselfish. In fact you *will* be unselfish; it won't be an effort on your part. Knowing yourself, you will know not only yourself but the self of everyone. It is the same; it is one consciousness, one continent. People are not islands. But without teaching people how to know their own being, Christianity has played a dangerous game, and one that has appealed to people because they have used a beautiful word, "unselfishness." It looks religious, it looks spiritual. When I say, "First be selfish," it does not look spiritual.

Selfish?

Your mind is conditioned that unselfishness is spiritual. I know it is, but unless you are selfish enough to know yourself, unselfishness is impossible. Unselfishness will come as a consequence of knowing yourself, of being yourself. Then unselfishness will not be an act of virtue, not done in order to gain rewards in heaven. Then unselfishness will simply be your nature, and each act of unselfishness will be a reward unto itself.

But Christianity has put the horse behind the cart—nothing is moving, everything has got stuck. The horses are stuck because the cart is in front of them, and the cart cannot move because no cart can move unless the horses are ahead of it, pulling it.

It happens to almost every Christian that when he or she starts to meditate, it brings a feeling of guilt—when the whole world is so troubled, when people are so poor, when people are dying of starvation, when people are suffering from AIDS, you are meditating? You must be utterly selfish! First help the poor, first help the people who are suffering from AIDS, first help everybody else.

But your life is very short. In seventy or eighty years, how many unselfish acts can you manage? And when are you going to find time for meditation—because whenever you start moving towards meditation those poor people are there, new diseases have sprung up, orphans are there beggars are there.

One mother was telling her small boy, "To be unselfish is a fundamental of our religion. Never be selfish, help others."

The little boy—and little boys are more perceptive and clear than your so-called old boys—the little boy said, "This seems to be a very strange thing, that I should help others and they should help me. Why not make it simple? I help myself, they help themselves." This fundamental of the religion seems to be very complicated—and unnecessarily complicated.

In fact, Christianity has condemned the Eastern religions for the simple reason that they look selfish. Mahavira, the Jain mystic, meditating for twelve years . . . he should be teaching in a school, or working in a hospital. He should look after orphans, be a Mother Teresa and get a Nobel prize.

It is clear that no meditator has ever received a Nobel prize. For what?—you have not done anything unselfish. You are the most selfish people in the world, just meditating and enjoying your silence and peace and blissfulness, finding the truth, finding godliness, becoming completely free from all prisons. This is all selfishness. So the Christian mind finds it a little difficult to accept the idea of meditation. In Christianity there is no meditation, only prayer.

They cannot call Gautam Buddha a really religious man, because what has he done for the poor? What has he done for the sick? What has he done for the old? He became enlightened—that is the ultimate in selfishness! But the East has a totally different outlook—and far more logical, reasonable, understandable. The East has always thought unless you have a peace, a silence in your heart, a song in your being, a light radiating your enlightenment, you cannot be of any service to anybody. You yourself are sick; you yourself are an orphan because you have not found yet the ultimate security of existence, the eternal safety of life. You are so poor yourself that inside there is nothing but darkness. How can you help others? You yourself are drowning, it will be dangerous to help others; most probably you will drown the other person also. First you have to learn swimming. Then only can you be of any help to someone who is drowning.

My approach is absolutely clear. First be selfish, and discover all that is contained in yourself—all the joys and all the blissfulness and all the ecstasies. And then unselfishness will come just like your shadow follows you—because to have a dancing heart, to have godliness in your being, you have to share it. You cannot go on keeping it like a miser, because miserliness in your inner growth is a death.

The economics of inner growth is different from the outer economics. The ordinary economics is that if you go on giving, you will have less and less and less. But the spiritual economics is that if you don't give, you will have less and less and less; if you give, you will have more and more and more. The laws of the outside world and the inside world are diametrically opposite.

First become rich inside, first become an emperor. Then you have so much to share, you will not even call it unselfishness. And you will not have the desire that some reward should be given to you, here or hereafter. You will not even ask for gratitude from the person you have given something to; on the contrary, you will be grateful that the person did not reject your love, your bliss, your ecstasy. The person was receptive, allowed you to pour your heart and your songs and your music into his being.

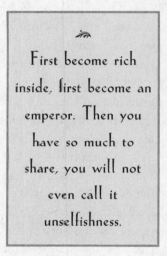

First become rich inside, first become an emperor. Then you have so much to share, you will not even call it unselfishness.

The Christian idea of unselfishness is sheer stupidity. The East has never thought in the same way. The whole history of the East and its search for truth is very long and it has found one simple fact—that first you have to take care of yourself, and then only you can take care of others.

The questioner feels a certain guilt. She says, "I seem to have to push through a layer of unease, guilt and confusion. Would you speak about it?"

It is a simple phenomenon. Christianity has deceived millions of people through a wrong path. And a fundamentalist Christian is the most fanatic, most bigoted person you can find. Nowadays the East has forgotten its own peaks of glory—the days of Gautam Buddha and Mahavira. Now even people who are not Christians are influenced by the Christian ideology. The Indian constitution nowadays says that charity consists of helping the poor, spreading education to the poor, and making hospitals for the poor. None of these three things will be found in the teachings of Gautam Buddha. Not that he is against helping the poor, but because he knows that if you are a meditator you *will* help, but you will not brag about it. It will be a simple, natural thing.

But to teach meditation is not charity, to open a hospital is charity. To open a school and teach geography and history is charity. And what are you going to teach in geography?—where is Timbuktu, where is Constantinople. In history, what are you going to teach?— about Genghis Khan, Tamerlane, Nadirshah, Alexander the Great, Ivan the Terrible. This is charity? But to teach people to be silent, peaceful, loving, joyous, contented, fulfilled is not charity. Even the people who are not Christians have become infected with the disease.

Mahatma Ghandi, at least three times in his life, was almost on the verge of becoming a Christian. In fact, he was a Christian, ninety percent. Dr. Ambedkar, who wrote the Indian constitution, had been thinking for years that he and his followers, the untouchables, should become Christians. Finally he decided that they should become Buddhists. But in the whole Indian constitution you can see the impact of Christianity. In the whole of the Indian constitution there is not even the mention of the word "meditation"—which has been the contribution of the East to the world, and its most precious contribution. Instead, the constitution reflects more what the Christian missionaries go on teaching. It does not reflect Gautam Buddha, it does not reflect Kabir, it does not reflect Nanak.

I cannot see that there can be any charity without meditation.

So your guilt is just a wrong conditioning. Drop it, without even giving it a second thought. You will become unselfish by being absolutely selfish. First you have to become inwardly rich—so rich, so overflowingly rich that you *have* to share, just as a rain cloud has to share its rain with the thirsty earth. But first the cloud must be full of rain. Saying to the empty clouds, "You should be unselfish," is just irrational.

People come to see me, well wishers, with good intentions, and they say, "This is a strange place you have around you. You should open a hospital for the poor; you should collect the orphans; you should distribute clothes to the beggars; you should help those who need help" My approach is totally different. I can distribute birth control methods to the poor so that there are no orphans. I can distribute the pill to the poor so there is no explosion of population because I don't see the point—first create the orphans and then create orphanages and then serve them and waste your life?

When I started speaking in the 1960s, India had a population of four hundred million. I have been saying since then that birth control is an absolute necessity. But the Christians are against birth control, and just within thirty-five years, India more than doubled its population. From four hundred million it went to nine hundred million. Five hundred million people could have been prevented, and there would have been no need of Mother Teresa, no need for the pope to come to India and teach unselfishness.

But people are strange—first let them become sick, then give medicine. And they have found beautiful ways. In every Lions Club and Rotary Club, they keep boxes for their members—if you purchase a bottle of some medicine and you are cured, and half the bottle is still there, you donate it to the Lions Club. This way they collect medicine, and then they are great, unselfish people so they are distributing the medicine. Service is their motto. But it is a very cunning service. Those medicines were going to be thrown away—if you are cured, what are you going to do with the remaining medicine? It is a great idea to collect all those medicines and distribute them to the poor—and have a great feeling of being public servants.

In my vision, the thing that man needs first and foremost is a meditative consciousness. And after you have your meditative consciousness, whatever you do will be helpful to everybody; you cannot do any harm, you can do only compassionate and loving acts.

So I repeat: first be selfish. Know thyself, be thyself and then your very life will be nothing but a sharing, an unselfish sharing, and without asking for any reward in this world or in the other world.

THE HEALING POWER
OF LOVE

❧

Everybody is brought up in such a way that everybody has become idealistic. Nobody is realistic. The ideal is the common
disease of humanity.

Everybody is brought up in such a way that everybody goes on
thinking that they have to be something, somebody, somewhere in
the future. An image is given and you have to be like it. That gives
you a tension because you are not it, you are something else, yet you
have to be it.

So one goes on condemning the real for the unreal—the unreal
is unreal. And the ideal goes on pulling you towards the future, out
of the present.

The ideal becomes a constant nightmare because it goes on condemning. Whatsoever you do is imperfect because you have an ideal
of perfection. Whatsoever you attain is still not fulfilling because you
have a mad expectation which can never be satisfied.

You are human, in a certain time, in a certain space, with certain
limitations. Accept those limitations. Perfectionists are always on the
brink of madness. They are obsessed people—whatsoever they do is
not good enough. And there is no way to do something perfectly—
perfection is not humanly possible. In fact, imperfect is the only way
to be.

126

So what do I teach you here? I don't teach you perfection, I teach you wholeness. That is a totally different thing. Be whole. Don't bother about perfection. When I say be whole, I mean be real, be here; whatsoever you do, do it totally. You will be imperfect but your imperfection will be full of beauty, it will be full of your totality.

Never try to be perfect otherwise you will create much anxiety. So many troubles are there already; don't create more troubles for yourself.

I have heard:

It happened that bedraggled, worried Garfinkel sat in a train holding a three-year-old boy. Every few minutes Garfinkel spanked the child.

"If you strike that baby one more time," said a woman sitting across from him, "I'll give you so much trouble you won't forget it!"

"Trouble?" said Garfinkel. "You're gonna give me trouble? Lady, my partner stole all my money and ran off with my wife and car. My daughter is in the parlor car, six months pregnant, and she ain't got no husband. My baggage is lost, I'm on the wrong train, and this little stinker just ate the tickets and threw up all over me. And lady, *you're* gonna give me trouble?"

> Be whole. Don't bother about perfection. When I say be whole, I mean be real, be here; whatsoever you do, do it totally. You will be imperfect but your imperfection will be full of beauty, it will be full of your totality.

Now what more trouble can there be? Don't you think enough is enough?

Life itself is so complicated, please be a little kinder towards yourself. Don't create ideals. Life is creating enough problems but those problems can be solved. If you are in a wrong train you can change the train; if the tickets are lost, they can be purchased again; if your wife has run away, you can find another woman. The problems that life gives to you can be solved but the problems that idealism gives to you can never be solved—they are impossible.

Somebody is trying to become Jesus . . . . Now there is no way; it does not happen that way, nature does not allow it. Jesus happens once, and only once; nature does not tolerate any repetition. Somebody is trying to become a Buddha—now he is trying to do the impossible. It simply does not happen, cannot happen; it is against nature. You can be only yourself. So be total. Wherever you are and whatsoever you are doing, do it totally. Move into it, let it become your meditation. Don't be worried whether it will be perfect or not—it is not going to be perfect. If it is total it is enough. If it was total you enjoyed doing it, you felt a fulfillment through it, you moved into it, you were absorbed into it, you came out of it new, fresh, young, rejuvenated.

Each act that is done totally rejuvenates, and each act that is done totally never brings any bondage. Love totally and attachment does not arise; love partially and attachment arises. Live totally and you are not afraid of death; live partially and you are afraid of death.

But forget the word "perfection." It is one of the most criminal words. This word should be dropped from all the languages of the world, it should be dropped from the human mind. Nobody has ever been perfect and nobody can ever be. Can't you see it? Even if God is there and you come to meet him, can't you find faults with his creation? So many, that's why he is hiding. He is almost afraid of you. Faults and faults and faults. Can you count them? Infinite faults you will find. In fact, if you are a fault-finder you cannot find anything right—in the right time, in the right place. Everything seems to be just a mess.

Even God is not perfect; God is total. He enjoyed doing it, he is still enjoying doing it. But he is not perfect. If he were perfect then the creation could not be imperfect. Out of perfection, perfection will come.

All the religions of the world say that God is perfect. I don't say so. I say God is whole, God is holy, God is total—but not perfect. Although he may still be trying . . . . How can he be perfect? If he were, the world would be dead by now. Once something is perfect, death happens because there is no future, there is no way. Trees are still growing, babies are still born—things continue. And he goes on improving. Can't you see the improvement? He goes on improving on everything. That's the meaning of evolution: things are being improved. Monkeys have become man—that's an improvement. Then man will become divine, will become a god himself—that is evolution.

Teilhard de Chardin says there is an omega point where everything will become perfect. There is none. There is no omega point. There cannot be. The world is always in the process; evolution is there; we are approaching and approaching but we never reach because once we reach—finished. God still goes on trying in different ways, improving.

One thing is certain: he is happy with his work, otherwise he would have abandoned it. He is still pouring his energy into it. When God is happy with you it is sheer nonsense to be unhappy with yourself. Be happy with yourself. Let happiness be the ultimate value. I am a hedonist. Always remember that happiness is the criterion. Whatsoever you do, be happy, that's all. Don't be bothered whether it is perfect or not.

Why this obsession with perfection? Then you will be tense, anxious, nervous, always uneasy, troubled, in conflict. The English word "agony" comes from a root which means "to be in conflict." To be constantly wrestling with oneself—that is the meaning of agony. You will be in agony if you are not at ease with yourself. Don't demand the impossible—be natural, at ease, loving yourself and loving others.

And remember, a person who cannot love himself because he goes on condemning himself cannot love anybody else either. A perfectionist is not only a perfectionist about himself, he is about others also. A man who is hard on himself is bound to be hard on others. His demands are impossible.

In India there was Mahatma Gandhi, a perfectionist, almost a neurotic. And he was very hard with his disciples—even tea was not allowed. Tea! Because it has caffeine. If somebody was found drinking tea in his ashram it was a great sin. Love was not allowed. If somebody fell in love with somebody it was such a great sin that it was as if the whole world was going to be drowned because of it. He was continuously spying on his disciples, always sitting at the keyhole. But he was that way with himself. You can be with others only as you are with yourself.

> ⤫
>
> Try to love yourself. Don't condemn. Once humanity starts having a deep acceptance, all the churches will disappear, and all politicians and priests will disappear.

But these types of people become great leaders because they create much guilt in others. The more guilt you can create in people the greater the leader you can become. Because more and more people feel that yes, you can help them to become perfect. They are imperfect so you can help them to become perfect.

I am not here to help you to become perfect; I am not concerned with any sort of nonsense. I am just here to help you to be yourself. If you are imperfect, beautiful; if you are perfect, that too is beautiful.

Don't try to become imperfect—because even that can become an ideal! You may be perfect already—then listening to me can create trouble for you! "This man says be imperfect"—there is no need. If you are perfect, accept that too!

Try to love yourself. Don't condemn. Once humanity starts having a deep acceptance, all the churches will disappear, and all politicians and priests will disappear.

I have heard:

A man was fishing in the North Woods and one night around the campfire his guide was telling him of the time he had guided Harry Emerson Fosdick on a fishing trip.

"Yes," said the guide, "he was a good man except for his swearing."

"But look," said the fisherman, "surely you don't mean to say that Dr. Fosdick was profane?"

"Oh, but he was, sir," protested the guide. "Once he caught a fine bass. Just as he was about to land him in the boat, the fish wiggled off the hook. So I say to the Doctor, 'That's a damned shame!' and the Doc comes right back and says, 'Yes, it is!' But that's the only time I ever heard him use such language."

Now, this is the mind of a perfectionist. The Doctor has not said anything! He simply says, "Yes, it is." But even that is enough for a perfectionist to find fault.

A perfectionist is neurotic. And not only is he neurotic, he creates neurotic trends around him. So don't be a perfectionist, and if somebody is a perfectionist around you escape as fast as you can before that person pollutes your mind.

All perfectionism is a sort of deep ego trip. Just to think of yourself in terms of ideals and perfection is nothing but to decorate your ego to its uttermost. A humble person accepts that life is not perfect. A humble person, a really religious person, accepts that we all have limitations.

That is my definition of humbleness. Not to try to be perfect is to be humble. And a humble person becomes more and more total, because he has nothing to deny, nothing to reject. He accepts whatever he is, good or bad. And a humble person is very rich because he accepts his wholeness; his anger, his sexuality, his greed—everything is accepted. In that deep acceptance a great alchemical change happens.

All that is ugly by and by disappears of its own accord. He becomes more and more harmonious, more and more whole.

I am not in favor of saints but I am in favor of those who are holy. A saint is a perfectionist; one who is holy is totally different. Zen Masters are holy; Catholic saints are saints. The very word "saint" is ugly. It comes from a word that means the person has been given sanction by the authority. Now, who can authorize anybody to be a saint, is it a sort of degree, a certificate? But the Church goes on doing that foolish thing. Even posthumous degrees are awarded! A saint may have died three hundred years ago, and then the Church revises its ideas. The world has changed, and after three hundred years the Church gives a posthumous degree—a sanction that the person was really a saint, we could not understand him at the time. And the church may have killed that person! That's how Joan of Arc became a saint; they killed her but later on they changed their minds. People by and by came closer and closer to Joan of Arc and it became difficult not to accept her. First they killed her, then they worshipped her. After hundreds of years, her bones were found and worshipped. She was burned by the same people, the same Church. No, the word "saint" is not good. A holy person is holy because of himself, because of herself, not because some church decides to award sainthood.

I have heard:

Jacobson, aged ninety, had lived through beatings in Polish pogroms, concentration camps in Germany, and dozens of other anti-Semitic experiences.

"Oh, Lord!" he prayed, sitting in a synagogue. "Is it true that we are your chosen people?"

And from the heavens boomed a voice: "Yes, Jacobson, the Jews are my chosen people!"

"Well, then," wailed the old man, "isn't it time you chose somebody else?"

Perfectionists are the chosen people of God, remember. In fact, the day you understand that you are creating your own misery because of your ideals, you break out of those ideals. Then you simply live from your reality, whatever it is. That is a great transformation.

Don't try to be the chosen people of God, just be human.

ONLY COMPASSION IS THERAPEUTIC

All that is ill in the human being is because of lack of love. All that is wrong with man is somewhere associated with love. He has not been able to love, or he has not been able to receive love. He has not been able to share his being. That's the misery. That creates all sorts of complexes inside.

Those wounds inside can surface in many ways. They can become physical illness, they can become mental illness—but deep down man suffers from lack of love. Just as food is needed for the body, love is needed for the soul. The body cannot survive without food, and the soul cannot survive without love. In fact, without love the soul is never born—there is no question of its survival.

You simply think that you have a soul; you believe that you have a soul because of your fear of death. But you have not known unless you have loved. Only in love does one come to feel that one is more than the body, more than the mind.

And only compassion is therapeutic. What is compassion? Compassion is the purest form of love. Sex is the lowest form of love, compassion the highest form of love. In sex the contact is basically physical; in compassion the contact is basically spiritual. In love, compassion and sex are mixed, the physical and the spiritual are mixed. Love is midway between sex and compassion.

You can call compassion meditation, also. The highest form of energy is compassion.

The word "compassion" is beautiful: half of it is "passion"—somehow passion has become so refined that it is no longer like passion. It has become compassion.

In sex, you use the other, you reduce the other to a means, you reduce the other to a thing. That's why in a sexual relationship you feel guilty. And that guilt is deeper than religious teachings. In a sexual relationship *as such* you feel guilty, and you feel guilty because you are reducing a human being to a thing, to a commodity to be used and thrown away.

That's why in sex you also feel a sort of bondage—you are also being reduced to a thing. And when you are a thing your freedom disappears, because your freedom exists only when you are a person. The more you are a person, the more free; the more you are a thing, the less free.

The furniture in your room is not free. If you leave the room locked and you come back after many years, the furniture will be in the same place, in the same way; it will not arrange itself in a new way. It has no freedom. But if you leave a person in the room, you will not find that person the same—not even the next day, not even the next moment. You cannot find the same person again. Says old Heraclitus, "You cannot step in the same river twice." You cannot come across the same person again. It is impossible to meet the same person twice because the human being is a river, continuously flowing. You never know what is going to happen. The future remains open.

For a *thing*, the future is closed. A rock will remain a rock will remain a rock. It has no potential for growth. It cannot change, it cannot evolve. A human being never remains the same—may fall back, may go ahead; may go into hell or into heaven, but never remains the same. Goes on moving, this way or that.

When you have a sexual relationship with somebody, you have reduced that somebody to a thing. And in reducing the other you have reduced yourself also to a thing, because it is a mutual compromise: "I allow you to reduce me to a thing, you allow me to reduce you to a thing. I allow you to use me, you allow me to use you. We use each other. We both have become things."

Watch two lovers—when they have not yet settled, when the

romance is still alive, the honeymoon has not ended, you will see two persons throbbing with life, ready to explode into the unknown. Then watch a married couple, a husband and the wife, and you will see two dead things, two graveyards side by side—helping each other to remain dead, forcing each other to remain dead. That is the constant conflict of the marriage. Nobody wants to be reduced to a thing!

Sex is the lowest form of that energy "X." If you are religious, call it "godliness"; if you are scientific, call it "X." This energy, X, can become love. When it becomes love, then you start respecting the other person. Yes, sometimes you use the other person but you feel thankful. You never say thank you to a thing. When you are in love with a woman and you make love to her, you say thank you. When you make love to your wife, have you ever said thank you? No, you take it for granted. Has your wife ever said thank you to you? Maybe, many years ago, you can remember some time when you were just undecided, were just courting, trying to seduce each other—maybe. But once you were settled, has she said thank you to you for anything? You have been doing so many things for her, she has been doing so many things for you. You are both living for each other—but gratitude has disappeared.

In love there is gratitude, there is a deep gratefulness. You know that the other is not a thing. You know that the other has a grandeur, a soul, an individuality. In love you give total freedom to the other. Of course, you give and you take; it is a give-and-take relationship—but with respect. In sex, it is a give-and-take relationship with no respect.

In compassion, you simply give. There is no idea anywhere in your mind to get anything back—you simply share. Not that nothing comes to you! A millionfold it is returned, but that is just by the way, just a natural consequence. There is no hankering for it.

In love, if you give something, deep down you go on expecting that it should be returned. If it is not returned, you feel like complaining. You may not say anything but in a thousand and one ways it can be inferred that you are grumbling, that you are feeling you have been cheated. Love seems to be a subtle bargain.

In compassion you simply give. In love, you are thankful because the other has given something to you. In compassion, you are thankful because the other has taken something from you; you are thankful because the other has not rejected you. You had come with energy to give, you had come with many flowers to share, and the other allowed you, the other was receptive. You are thankful because the other was receptive.

Compassion is the highest form of love. Much comes back—a millionfold, I say—but that is not the point, you don't hanker for it. If it is not coming there is no complaint about it. If it is coming you are simply surprised! If it is coming, it is unbelievable. If it is not coming there is no problem—you had never given your heart to anybody as part of any bargain. You simply shower because you have. You have so much that if you don't shower you will become burdened. Just like a cloud full of rainwater has to shower. And next time when a cloud is showering watch silently, and you will always hear—when the cloud has showered and the earth has absorbed, you will always hear the cloud saying to the earth, "Thank you." The earth helped the cloud to unburden.

> In compassion, you simply give. There is no idea anywhere in your mind to get anything back—you simply share.

When a flower has bloomed, it has to release its fragrance to the winds. It is natural! It is not a bargain, it is not a business—it is simply natural! The flower is full of fragrance—what to do? If the flower keeps the fragrance to itself then the flower will feel very, very tense, in deep anguish. The greatest anguish in life is when you cannot express, when you cannot communicate, when you cannot share. The poorest person is one who has nothing to share, or who has something to share but has lost the capacity, the art, of how to share it—then a person is poor.

The sexual man is very poor. The loving man is richer, comparatively. The man of compassion is the richest—at the top of the world. He has no confinement, no limitation. He simply gives and goes on his way. He does not even wait for you to say thank you. With tremendous love he shares his energy.

This is what I call therapeutic.

Christians believe that Jesus did many miracles. I cannot see him doing any miracle. The miracle was his compassion. If anything happened, it happened without his doing it. If anything ever happens in the highest plane of being, it always happens without any effort. He moved; many sorts of people came to him. He was there like a tremendous pool of energy—anybody who was ready to share, shared.

Miracles happened! He was therapeutic. He was one of the greatest healers the world has ever known. Buddha, or Mahavira, or Krishna—they are all great healers on different levels. Yes, you cannot find in Buddha's life any miracle of healing an ill person, or healing a blind man, or bringing a dead person to life. You will be surprised: Was Jesus's compassion greater than Buddha's? What happened? Why were many people not healed through Buddha's energy? No, it is not a question of more or less. Buddha's compassion functioned on a different level. He had a different type of audience than Jesus, and a different type of people around him.

It always happens—almost always—I go on watching as the stream of people comes to me from the West. They never ask anything about their bodies. They don't come to me and say, "I have a constant headache, Osho, help me, do something!" Or, "My eyes are weak," or, "My concentration is not good," or, "My memory is going bad"—no, never. But the Indians come and always bring something of the physical. Mm? They have had an upset stomach for many years—"Osho, do something!"

Almost always I feel: Why? What has happened to India? Why do these people come only for some bodily, physical problems? They have only those problems. A poor country, a very poor country, has no spiritual problems. A rich country has spiritual problems; a poor country has physical problems.

Buddha's time in India was its golden age. That was the time when India was at its peak. The country was rich, tremendously rich, affluent. The rest of the world was poor, and India was very rich. The people coming to Buddha were bringing spiritual problems. Yes, they were also bringing wounds, but theirs were spiritual wounds.

Jesus moved around in a very poor country, lived in a very poor country. The people who were coming to him had no spiritual problems, in fact, because to have a spiritual problem you have to attain a certain standard of living. Otherwise, your problems are concerned with the lower levels. A poor man has different kinds of problems.

One of my relatives was here for one month—he was meditating, doing things, and on the last day of his visit I was hoping he would ask something meaningful. What did he ask? He said that his son is not doing well financially. Living for one month here, listening to me for one month, and this was the only question that came to his mind: his son is not doing well. He drives a taxi, and the car they have purchased is such that every day there is some problem or other—he asked me, "Osho, do something!"

I am not a car mechanic! So I told him, "Sell the car and get another one." He said, "Nobody will purchase it, so please—do something!"

When people are poor, their problems are of the world. When people are rich, their problems are of a higher quality. Only an affluent country can be really spiritual; a poor country cannot be.

I am not saying that a poor individual cannot be—yes, a poor person can be really spiritual, exceptions are there—but a poor country cannot be. A poor country, on the whole, thinks in terms of money, medicine, houses, cars, this and that. And it is natural, it is logical!

Jesus moved in a very poor world. People were seeking their own solutions. Many were helped—not that Jesus was helping but they were helped. And Jesus says again and again: "It is your faith that has healed you." When you have faith, compassion can pour into you. When you have faith, you are open to compassion. Buddha did miracles, but those miracles are of the invisible. Mahavira did miracles, but those miracles are of the invisible. You cannot see them—they can only be seen by the person to whom they have happened.

But compassion is always therapeutic; whatever your level, it helps you. Compassion is love purified—so much so that you simply give and don't ask anything in return.

Buddha used to say to his disciples, "After each meditation, be compassionate—immediately—because when you meditate, love grows, the heart becomes full. After each meditation, feel compassion for the whole world so that you share your love and you release the energy into the atmosphere and that energy can be used by others."

I would also like to say that to you: After each meditation, when you are celebrating, have compassion. Just feel that your energy should go and help people in whatsoever ways they need it. Just release it! You will be unburdened, you will feel very relaxed, you will feel very calm and quiet, and the vibrations that you have released will help many. End your meditations always with compassion.

And compassion is unconditional. You cannot have compassion only for those who are friendly towards you, only for those who are related to you.

It happened in China:

When Bodhidharma went to China, a man came to him. He said, "I have followed your teachings: I meditate and then I feel compassion for the whole universe—not only for men, but for animals, for rocks and rivers also. But there is one problem: I cannot feel compassion for my neighbor. No—it is impossible! So you please tell me: can I exclude my neighbor from my compassion? I include the whole existence, known and unknown, but can I exclude my neighbor?—because it is very difficult, impossible. I cannot feel compassion for him."

Bodhidharma said, "Then forget about meditation, because if compassion excludes anybody then it is no longer there."

Compassion is all-inclusive—intrinsically all-inclusive. So if you cannot feel compassion for your neighbor, then forget all about it—because it has nothing to do with somebody in particular. It has something to do with your inner state. *Be* compassion—unconditionally, undirected, unaddressed. Then you become a healing force in this world of misery.

Jesus says: "Love thy neighbor as thyself"—again and again. And he also says: "Love thine enemy as thyself." If you analyze both sentences together, you will come to find that the neighbor and the enemy are almost always the same person! "Love thy neighbor as thyself" and "Love thine enemy as thyself."

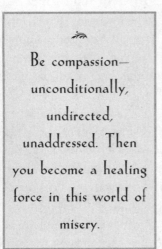

Be compassion—
unconditionally,
undirected,
unaddressed. Then
you become a healing
force in this world of
misery.

What does he mean?

He simply means: don't have any barriers for your compassion, for your love. As you love yourself, love the whole existence—because in the ultimate analysis the whole existence is you, reflected in many mirrors. It is you—it is not separate from you. Your neighbor is just a form of you; your enemy is also a form of you. Whatever you come across, you come across yourself. You may not recognize it because you are not very alert; you may not be able to see yourself in the other, but then something is wrong with your vision, something is wrong with your eyes.

Compassion is therapeutic. And to be compassionate one has to have compassion for oneself in the first place. If you don't love yourself you will never be able to love anybody else. If you are not kind to yourself you cannot be kind to anybody else. Your so-called saints, who are so very hard on themselves, are just pretending that they are kind to others. It is not possible; psychologically it is impossible. If you cannot be kind to yourself, how can you be kind to others?

Whatever you are with yourself, you are with others. Let that be a basic understanding. If you hate yourself you will hate others—and you have been taught to hate yourself. Nobody has ever said to you, "Love yourself!" The very idea seems absurd—loving oneself? The very idea makes no sense—loving oneself? We always think that to love, one needs somebody else. But if you don't learn it with yourself you will not be able to practice it with others.

You have been told, constantly conditioned, that you are not of any worth. From every direction you have been shown, you have been told that you are unworthy, that you are not what you should be, that you are not accepted as you are. There are many shoulds hanging over your head—and those shoulds are almost impossible to fulfill. And when you cannot fulfill them, when you fall short, you feel condemned. A deep hatred arises in you about yourself.

How can you love others? So full of hatred, where are you going to find love? So you only pretend, you only show that you are in love. Deep down you are not in love with anybody—you cannot be. Those pretensions are good for a few days, then the color disappears, then reality asserts itself.

Every love affair is on the rocks. Sooner or later, every love affair becomes poisoned. How does it become so poisoned? Both people pretend that they are loving, both go on saying that they love. The father says he loves the child; the child says he loves the father. The mother says she loves her daughter and the daughter goes on saying the same thing. Brothers say they love each other. The whole world talks about love, sings about love—and can you find any other place so loveless? Not an iota of love exists—only mountains of talk, Himalayas of poetry about love.

It seems all these poetries are just compensations. Because we cannot love, we have somehow to believe through poetry, through singing, that we love. What we miss in life we put into our poetry. What we go on missing in life, we put into the film, in the novel. Love is absolutely absent, because the first step has not been taken yet.

The first step is to accept yourself as you are; drop all shoulds. Don't carry any "ought" in your heart! You are not to be somebody else; you are not expected to do something that doesn't belong to you—you are just to be yourself. Relax, and just be yourself. Be respectful to your individuality and have the courage to sign your own signature. Don't go on copying others' signatures.

You are not expected to become a Jesus or a Buddha or a Ramakrishna—you are simply expected to become yourself. It was good that Ramakrishna never tried to become somebody else, so he became Ramakrishna. It was good that Jesus never tried to become like Abraham or Moses, so he became Jesus. It is good that Buddha never tried to become a Patanjali or Krishna—that's why he became a Buddha.

When you are not trying to become anybody else, then you simply relax—then a grace arises. Then you are full of grandeur, splendor, harmony—because then there is no conflict, nowhere to go, nothing to fight for; nothing to enforce upon yourself violently. You become innocent. In that innocence you will feel compassion and love for yourself. You will feel so happy with yourself that even if God comes and knocks at your door and says, "Would you like to become somebody else?" you will say, "Have you gone mad?! I am perfect! Thank you, but never try anything like that—I am perfect as I am."

The moment you can say to existence, "I am perfect as I am, I am happy as I am," this is what in the East we call *shraddha*, trust. Then you have accepted yourself, and in accepting yourself you have accepted existence.

Denying yourself you deny the existence that created you. The moment you say, "I should be like this," you are trying to improve upon existence. You are saying, "You committed blunders—I should have been like this, and you have made me like this?" You are trying to improve upon existence. It is not possible. Your struggle is in vain—you are doomed to failure.

And the more you fail, the more you hate. The more you fail, the more you feel condemned. The more you fail, the more you feel yourself impotent. And out of this hatred, impotency, how can compassion arise? Compassion arises when you are perfectly grounded in your being. You say, "Yes, this is the way I am." You have no ideals to fulfill. And immediately fulfillment starts happening!

The roses bloom so beautifully because they are not trying to become lotuses. And the lotuses bloom so beautifully because they have not heard any legends about other flowers. Everything in nature goes so beautifully in accord, because nobody is trying to compete with anybody, nobody is trying to become anybody else. Everything is the way it is.

> Compassion arises when you are perfectly grounded in your being. You say, "Yes, this is the way I am." You have no ideals to fulfill.

Just see the point! Just be yourself and remember you cannot be anything else, whatsoever you do. All effort is futile. You have to be just yourself.

There are only two ways. One is that by rejecting, you can remain the same; condemning, you can remain the same. Or accepting, surrendering, enjoying, delighting, you can be the same. Your attitude can be different, but you are going to remain the way you are, the person you are. Once you accept, compassion arises. And then you start accepting others!

Have you watched it?—it is very difficult to live with a saint, very difficult. You can live with a sinner but you cannot live with a saint—because a saint will be condemning you continuously: with his gestures, with his eyes, the way he looks at you, the way he talks at you. A saint never talks *with* you—he talks *at* you. He never just looks at you; he always has some ideals in his eyes, clouding his vision. He never sees *you*. He has something far away in his mind, and he goes on comparing you with it—and, of course, you always fall short. His very look makes you a sinner! It is very difficult to live with a saint—because he does not accept himself, how can he accept you? He has many things in him, jarring notes that he feels he has to go beyond. Of course, he sees the same things in you in a magnified way.

But to me, only that person is a saint who has accepted himself, and in his acceptance has accepted the whole world. To me, that state of mind is what sainthood is: the state of total acceptance. And that is healing, therapeutic. Just being with somebody who accepts you totally is therapeutic. You will be healed.

So move slowly, alert, watching, be loving. If you are sexual I don't say drop sex: I say make it more alert, make it more prayerful, make it more profound, so that it can become love. If you are loving, then make it even more grateful; bring deeper gratitude, joy, celebration, meditation to it, so that it can become compassion.

Unless compassion has happened to you, don't think that you have lived rightly or that you have lived at all. Compassion is the flowering. And when compassion happens to one person, millions are healed. Whoever comes around him is healed.

Compassion is therapeutic.

UNCONDITIONALLY VALUE-FREE: THE COMPASSION OF ZEN

One evening as Shichiri Kojun was reciting sutras, a thief with a sharp sword entered, demanding either his money or his life.

Shichiri said to him, "Do not disturb me. You can find the money in that drawer." Then he resumed his recitation.

A little while afterwards he stopped and called, "Don't take it all. I need some to pay taxes with tomorrow."

The intruder gathered up most of the money and started to leave. "Thank a person when you receive a gift," Shichiri added. The man thanked him and made off.

A few days afterwards the fellow was caught, and confessed, among others, the offense against Shichiri. When Shichiri was called as a witness he said, "This man is no thief, at least as far as I am concerned. I gave him the money and he thanked me for it." After he had finished his prison term, the man went to Shichiri and became his disciple.

Jesus says, "Judge ye not." This was perfect Zen, had he stopped there. But maybe because he was talking to the Jews and he had to talk in a Jewish way, he added, ". . . so that you are not judged." Now it is no longer Zen. Now it is a bargain. That addition destroyed its very quality, its very depth.

"Judge ye not" is enough unto itself; nothing is needed to be added to it. "Judge ye not" means be non-judgmental. "Judge ye not" means look at life without any valuation. Don't evaluate—don't say "this is good" and don't say "this is bad." Don't be moralistic—don't call something divine, and don't call something evil. "Judge ye not" is a great statement that there is no God and no Devil.

Had Jesus stopped there, this small saying—only three words, "judge ye not"—would have transformed the whole character of Christianity. But he added something and destroyed it. He said, ". . . so that you are not judged." Now it becomes conditional. Now it is no longer non-judgmental, it is a simple bargain—"so that you are not judged." It is businesslike.

Out of the fear—so that you are not judged—don't judge. But

how can you drop judgment out of fear, or out of greed? So that you are not judged, don't judge—but greed and fear cannot make you value-free. It is self-centered—"Judge ye not, so that you are not judged." It is egoistic. The whole beauty of the saying is destroyed. The Zen flavor disappears, it becomes ordinary. It becomes good advice. It has no revolution in it; it is parental advice. Very good advice, but nothing radical. The second clause is a crucifixion of the radical statement.

Zen stops there: Judge ye not. Because Zen says all is as it is— nothing is good, nothing is bad. Things are the way they are. Some tree is tall and some tree is small. Somebody is moral and somebody is immoral. Somebody is praying and somebody has gone to steal. That's the way things are. Now, see the revolutionary flavor of it! It will make you afraid, it will frighten you. That's why Zen has no commandments. It does not say: Do this and don't do that—it has no shoulds and no should-nots. It has not created that prison of the "ought."

Zen is not perfectionistic. And now psychoanalysis knows well that perfectionism is a kind of neurosis. Zen is the only religion which is not neurotic. It accepts. Its acceptance is so total, so utterly total, that it will not even call a thief a thief, that it will not even call a murderer a murderer. Try to see the purity of its spirit—try to see the utter transcendence. All is as it is.

Zen is unconditionally value-free—if you make a condition, you miss the point. Zen has no fear and no greed. Zen has no God and no Devil, and Zen has no heaven and no hell. It does not make people greedy by alluring them, promising them rewards in heaven. And it does not make people frightened, scared, by creating nightmarish conceptions of hell.

It does not bribe you with rewards, and it does not punish you with tortures. It simply gives you an insight to see into things—and that insight frees you. That insight has no greed as a base to it and no fear as a base to it. All other religions are greedy, all other religions are based deep down somewhere in fear. That's why we use the word "god-fearing" for a religious person—a religious person is god-fearing.

But how can fear be religious? It is impossible. Fear can never be religious—only fearlessness. But if you have the idea of good and bad, you can never be fearless. Your ideas of good and bad make people feel guilty, make people cripples, make people paralyzed. How can you help them to be free from all fear?—impossible. You create *more* fear.

Ordinarily, a man who is not religious is less afraid, has less quantity of fear in his being than the so-called religious. The so-called religious is continuously trembling inside, continuously anxious about whether he is going to make it or he is going to lose it. Is he going to be thrown into hell? Or will he be able to do the impossible and enter paradise?

Even when Jesus is taking his last leave from his friends and disciples, the disciples are more worried about what their places will be in heaven. They will be meeting next in heaven—what will be their places? Who will be who? Of course, they concede Jesus will be just on the right hand of God—then who is going to be next to him? Their worry comes out of their greed and their fear. They are not much concerned that Jesus is going to be crucified tomorrow, they are much more concerned with their own interests.

All other religions are based in very ordinary greed and fear. The same greed that you have for money one day becomes transformed into the greed for God. Then, God is your money; now, money is your God—that's the only difference. Then God becomes your money. Now you are afraid of the state, of the police, of this and that—and then you start being afraid of hell, and the supreme court, the ultimate supreme court of God, the last day of judgment.

The so-called Christian saints, even in their last moments of life, are constantly trembling, afraid—are they going to make it or not?

Zen is unconditionally value-free. Let it sink in you very deeply, because that is my standpoint, too. I want you to understand, that's all. Understanding is enough. Let understanding be the only law; there is no other. Don't move according to fear, otherwise you will move in darkness. And don't move according to greed—because greed is nothing but fear upside down. They are two aspects of the same thing: on one side it is greed, on another side it is fear. A man who is fearful is always greedy, a man who is greedy is always fearful. They remain together, they go together.

Only understanding, only awareness, only the capacity to see into things as they are . . . Can't you accept existence as it is? And by not accepting it, nothing has been changed. What has been changed? For thousands of years we have been rejecting many things—they are still there, even more so. Thieves have not disappeared. Neither have murderers disappeared. Nothing has changed; things are exactly as they have been always. Prisons go on increasing. Laws go on growing and becoming more and more complicated. And because of the complicated laws, more and more thieves are employed—the lawyers, the judges . . . . It makes no change anywhere. Your whole prison system has not done any good—in fact it has been very harmful. The prison system has become the very university for crime—to learn crime, to learn crime from masters.

Once a man goes to prison, he becomes a constant visitor. Once he has been in prison, then again and again he goes back. It is very rare to find a man who has been to prison and who never goes back again. He comes out of prison more skillful. He comes out of prison with more ideas—how to do the same thing, now in a more expert way. He comes out of prison less amateurish. He comes out of prison with a degree; the release from prison is a kind of graduation into crime. Now he knows more, knows how to do it better. Now he knows how not to get caught. Now he knows what the loopholes are in the legal system.

And those who enforce law are as criminal as anybody else—in fact they have to be *more* criminal. They have to deal with criminals, so they have to be more criminal. The police and the prison guards and the jailers, they are more criminal than the people they are forcing into imprisonment—they have to be.

Nothing changes. This is not the way to change things, it has proved an utter failure. Zen says change comes through understanding, not by enforcing anything.

And what is your heaven and hell? Nothing but the same idea, transported beyond life. The same idea of prison becomes your idea of hell. And the same idea of reward—governmental rewards, presidential rewards, gold medals, this and that—that same idea becomes transported as heaven, paradise, *firdaus*. But the psychology is the same.

Zen destroys that psychology from the very root. Zen has no condemnation for anything. It has only understanding: it says try to understand things as they are. Try to understand man as he is—don't impose an ideal, don't say how he should be.

The moment you say how man should be, you become blind to the reality that he is. The 'should' becomes a barrier. Then you can't see the real, then you can't see that which is—your 'should' becomes too heavy. You have an ideal, a perfectionist ideal, and every person falls below it, naturally. Then everybody is condemned.

And those egoistic people who can manage somehow to force themselves into these ideals—at least superficially, at least outwardly—they become great saints. They are nothing but great egoists. And if you look into their eyes, just one flavor you will find: holier-than-thou. They are the chosen few, they are the chosen people of God and they are here to condemn you and to transform you.

Zen is not interested in anybody's transformation. And it transforms—that is the paradox. It is not concerned with how you should be, it is only concerned with what you are. See into it, see into it with loving, caring eyes. Try to understand what it is, and out of this understanding a transformation comes. The transformation is natural—you have not to do it, it simply happens on its own accord.

Zen transforms, but it doesn't talk about transformation. It changes, but it is not concerned with change. It brings more beatitude to human beings than anything else, but it is not concerned with that at all. It comes as a grace, as a gift. It follows understanding. That is the beauty of Zen, it is unconditionally value-free. Valuation is the disease of the mind—that's what Zen says. Nothing is good and nothing is bad, things are just as they are. Everything is as it is.

> Zen transforms, but it doesn't talk about transformation. It changes, but it is not concerned with change. It brings more beatitude to human beings than anything else, but it is not concerned with that at all.

In Zen a totally new dimension opens, the dimension of effortless transformation. The dimension of transformation that comes naturally with clearer eyes, with clarity. By seeing into the nature of things more directly, without any hindrance of prejudices.

The moment you say a man is good, you have stopped looking at him. You have labeled him already; you have pigeonholed him, you have categorized him. The moment you say "this man is bad" how can you look into his eyes anymore? You have decided offhand, you are finished with this person. This person is no longer a mystery. You have solved the mystery; you have written on it "this is bad" and "this is good." Now you will be interacting with these labels, and not the realities.

The good man can turn into bad, the bad man can turn into good. It is happening every moment—in the morning the man was good, by the evening he is bad, by the night he is again good. But now you will behave according to the labeling. You will not be talking to the man himself, you will be talking to your own label, to your own image.

Of course, you go on missing realities, real persons. And it creates a thousand and one complexities and problems. Unsolvable problems. Do you talk to your wife, really? When you are in bed with your wife, are you really in bed with your wife, or with a certain image? This is my feeling—that wherever two persons are meeting, there is a crowd really, not two persons. At least four persons certainly are there. Your image of the other and the other's image of you, those two images are there. And they never fit—the real person goes on changing, the real person is a flux. The real person is a river that goes on changing its color. The real person is alive! Just because you label the person does not mean he has gone dead—he is still alive.

Once somebody asked Chuang Tzu, "Is your work finished?" He said, "How can it be finished?—because I am still alive!"

See into it: he says, "How can it be finished? I am still alive. It can only be finished the day I am dead. I am still flowing, things will still go on happening."

When a tree is alive, flowers will come, new leaves will come, new birds will come and make their nests on it, new travelers will come and stay overnight under it . . . things will go on changing. Everything remains possible when you are alive. But the moment you label a person as good, bad, moral, immoral, religious, irreligious, theist, atheist, this and that—you are thinking as if the person has become dead. You should label only when a person is dead. You can label a person on the grave, not before it. You can go to the grave and you can write: "This person is this." Now he cannot contradict you; now things have finished, things have come to a stop. The river flows no more.

But while someone is alive . . . And we go on labeling—even children, small children. We say, "This child is obedient, and this child is very disobedient. This child is such a joy, and this child is such a problem." You label—and remember, when you label you create many problems. First, if you label somebody you support him to

151

behave the way you label him—because he starts feeling that now he is under an obligation to prove that you are right. If the father says, "My child is a problem," now the child thinks, "I have to prove that I am a problem, otherwise my father will be proved wrong." This reasoning is a very unconscious thing—how can a child believe his is father wrong? So he creates more problems, and the father says, "Look. The child is a problem."

> ❧
>
> Everything remains possible when you are alive. But the moment you label a person as good, bad, moral, immoral, religious, irreligious, theist, atheist, this and that—you are thinking as if the person has become dead. You should label only when a person is dead.

Three women were talking and, as women do, they were bragging about their children. One said, "My child is only five years old but he writes poetry. And such beautiful poetry that even accomplished poets will feel ashamed."

The second said, "This is nothing. My child is only four, and he paints—such modern, ultra-modern paintings, even Picasso cannot make any head or tail of it, what it is. And he does not use a brush, he simply uses his hands. Sometimes he simply throws the paint on the canvas and a beautiful thing, something out of the blue, arises. My child is an impressionist, a very original painter."

The third woman said, "This is nothing. My child is only three, and he goes to the psychoanalyst by himself."

If you label, you will manage to drive the child crazy . . . you will destroy him. All labels are destructive. Never label a person as a sinner or a saint. When too many people label a person in one way . . . And people tend to think collectively; people don't have individual, original ideas. Mm? You hear a rumor that somebody is a sinner and you accept it. And then you hand it over to somebody else, and he accepts it. And the rumor goes on growing, the label becomes bigger and bigger and bigger. And one day on that man the label "SINNER" is written in such big capital letters, in such neon signs, that he reads it himself and has to behave accordingly. The whole society expects him to be that way, otherwise people will be angry—"What are you doing? You are a sinner, and trying to be a saint! Behave yourself!"

That's what the society has—a very subtle investment in its labeling: "Behave yourself! Don't do anything that goes against our ideas of you." That is a tacit thing, but it is there.

Secondly, when you label a person, howsoever he tries to behave according to the label, he cannot. He cannot do it perfectly, it is impossible. It cannot be done really, he can only pretend. And then sometime or other when he is not pretending, when he is a little relaxed—he is in a holiday mood and he is on a picnic—the reality asserts. Then you think you have been deceived; this man is a deceiver. You were thinking he was good, and today he has stolen money from you. For years you have been thinking he was good, he was a saint—and now he has stolen money from you!

You think he has deceived you? No, it is your labeling that has deceived you. He is moving according to his reality. For long enough he tried to fit within your frame, but one day or other one grows out of the frame. One has to do things one wants to do.

Nobody is here to fulfill your expectations. And only very cowardly people try to fulfill others' expectations. A real man will destroy all people's expectations about him, because he is not here to be imprisoned by anybody's ideas. He will remain free. He will remain inconsistent—that is what freedom is. He will do one thing today, and he will do something exactly opposite tomorrow, so that you cannot carry an idea about him. A real, genuine human being is inconsistent. Only bogus people are consistent. A real, genuine human being carries contradictions within him. He is utter freedom. He is such a freedom that he can be this and he can be that too, just the opposite too. It is his choice—if he wants to be a leftist he is a leftist, if he wants to be a rightist he becomes a rightist. There is no hindrance in him. If he wants to be inside he can be inside, if he wants to be outside he can be outside. He is free. He can be an extrovert, he can be an introvert, he can do whatsoever. His freedom chooses in the moment what to do.

But we force a pattern on people that they should be consistent. There is great value put on consistency. We say, "This man is so consistent. This man is great—he is so consistent." But what do you mean by "consistency"? Consistency means the man is dead, he lives no more. He stopped living the day he became consistent—since then he has not lived.

When you say, "My husband is trustworthy," what do you mean? He has stopped loving, he has stopped living—now no other woman attracts him. If no other woman attracts him, how can you go on attracting him?—you are a woman. In fact, now he pretends. If the man is still living and loving, when he sees a beautiful woman he is attracted. When a woman is living and alive and kicking, when she sees a beautiful man, how is it that she will not feel attracted? It is so natural! I am not saying she has to go with him—but the attraction is natural. She may choose not to go—but to deny the attraction is to deny life itself.

Zen says: Remain true to your freedom. And then a totally different kind of being arises in you, which is very unexpected, unpredictable. Religious, but not moral. Not immoral—amoral: beyond morality, beyond immorality.

This is a new dimension that Zen opens into life. It is altogether a separate reality in which you have lived—this is totally separate from that. It has a new quality; the quality is that of characterlessness.

Sometimes this word hurts very much, because we have loved the word "character" too long. We have been conditioned for centuries for the word "character." We say, "That man is a man of character."

But have you watched? A man of character is a dead man. A man of character is categorizable, the man of character is predictable. The man of character has no future, has only the past.

Listen: The man of character has only his past. Because character means the past. He goes on repeating his past, he is a broken gramophone record. He goes on repeating the same thing again and again and again. He has nothing new to say. He has nothing new to live, he has nothing new to be. We call that man a man of character. You can rely on him, you can depend on him. He will not break his promises—yes, that is true. He has great utility, the social utility is great but that man is dead, that man is a machine.

Machines have characters; you can depend on them. That's why we are going to remove, by and by, all human beings and replace them with machines. Machines are more predictable, they have greater characters—you can depend on them.

A horse is not so dependable as a car. A horse has a kind of personality—some day he is not in the mood, and another day he does not want to go the way you want to go, and one day he is very rebellious. And some day he simply stands there and will not move. He has a soul; you cannot always depend on him. But a car has no soul. It is just put together; it has no center. It simply goes the way you want it to go. Even if you want the car to go over the cliff, it will go. The horse will say, "Wait! If you want to commit suicide, you can do it, but I am not taking it. You can jump. I am not jumping." But the car will not say no, it has no soul to say no. It never says yes, it never says no.

Sometimes even the mind of a great mathematician simply won't work. But the computer goes on working twenty-four hours—day in, day out, year in, year out—there is no question of not working. A machine has character, a very dependable character. And that's what we have been trying to do. First we tried to make man a machine; we could not succeed in it a hundred percent, so by and by we started to invent machines so that they could replace people. Sooner or later, people will be replaced everywhere. Machines will do far better, far more efficiently, more reliably, faster.

A man has moods because a man has a soul. Because man has a soul, he can only be authentic if he remains without a character. What do I mean when I say "characterless"? I mean the man goes on dropping his past. He does not live according to his past—that's why he is unpredictable. He lives moment to moment, he lives in the present. He looks around and he lives, he sees what is around him and he lives, he feels what is around and he lives. He has no fixed ideas of how to live; he has only awareness. His life remains a constant flow. He has spontaneity—that's what I mean when I say a real man is characterless. He has spontaneity.

He is responsive. If you say something to him, he responds to it, he does not repeat a cliché. He responds to you—to *this* moment, to *this* question, to *this* situation. He is not responding to some other, learned situation. He responds to you, he looks into you. He is not reacting, he is responding. A reaction comes out of the past.

It happened: A Zen master asked, "What is the secret of Buddha? What did he deliver to Mahakashyapa when he gave him the flower? Why did he say, 'I give to Mahakashyapa what I have not been able to give to anybody else—because others can understand only words, Mahakashyapa can understand silence'?"

Buddha had come that day with a lotus flower in his hand. All his disciples looked and looked, and they were worried and they started getting more and more restless. He would not say anything, he was looking at the lotus . . . as if he had forgotten the whole assembly. Minutes passed, and the hour was passing, and people got very fidgety. And then Mahakashyapa started laughing. Buddha called him and he gave the flower to him and he said, "What I can give through words, I have given to others. What I cannot give through words, I give it to you, Mahakashyapa. Keep it till you find a man who can receive the message in silence."

A Zen master asked his disciples, "What was the secret? What was given through the lotus? What happened in that moment?" A disciple stood, danced, ran out. And the master said, "Right. Exactly this is what it is."

But another master in the same monastery came to see this master in the night and said, "You should not agree so soon; your agreement was too early, I suspect."

So the master went to the disciple who had danced and to whom he had said, "Yes, this is it." In the night he went there and he asked the same question again: "What was it that Buddha gave in the lotus to Mahakashyapa? What was it that Mahakashyapa understood when he smiled? What was it? Tell me the answer."

The young man danced. And the master hit him hard! He said, "This is wrong, absolutely wrong."

The disciple said, "But just this morning you said it was right."

And the master said, "Yes. In the morning it was right, in the night it is wrong. You are repeating. In the morning I thought it was a response. Now I know it was a reaction."

The answer has to change, if it is a response, each time the question is put. The question may be the same but nothing else is the same. In the morning when the master asked, the sun was rising and the birds were singing, and the assembly . . . a thousand monks were sitting in meditation—it was a totally different kind of world. Yes, the question was the same, the linguistic formulation was the same. But the whole has changed, the gestalt has changed. In the night it is totally different; the master is alone with the disciple in his cell. The sun is no more there in the sky, and birds are no more singing, and there is nobody else to see. The master has changed. These few hours, the river has flowed on, has entered new pastures, has entered new territories. The question only *appears* to be the same. But the disciple got fixed. He thought, "So I know the answer."

No, in real life nobody knows the answers. In real life you have to be responsive. In real life you cannot carry answers ready-made, fixed, clichés. In real life you have to be open. That disciple missed.

A characterless man is a man who has no answers, who has no philosophy, who has no particular idea how things should be. Howsoever they are, he remains open. He is a mirror—he reflects.

Have you not watched? If you go before the mirror, if you are angry the mirror reflects your angry face; if you are laughing the mirror reflects your laughing face. If you are old the mirror reflects your old age, if you are young the mirror reflects your youth. You cannot say to the mirror, "Yesterday you reflected me laughing, and today you are reflecting me so angry and sad? What do you mean? You are inconsistent. You don't have any character! I will throw you out of the house."

The mirror has no character. And the real man is like a mirror.

Zen is non-judgmental, Zen is non-evaluative, Zen imposes no character on anybody. Because to impose character, you will need an evaluation—good or bad. To impose character you will have to create shoulds and should-nots; you will have to give commandments. To impose character you will have to be a Moses—you cannot be a Bodhidharma. To impose character you will have to create fear and greed. Otherwise who will listen to you? You will have to be a B. F. Skinner and treat people like rats—train them, punish them, reward them, so that they are forced into a certain pattern.

That's what has been done to you. Your parents have done it, your education has done it, your society, state, has done it. Zen says: Now it is enough, get out of it. Drop all this nonsense, start being yourself. That does not mean that Zen leaves you in chaos. No, just the opposite. Zen, instead of giving you a character, and a conscience to manipulate the character, gives you consciousness.

This difference has to be noted, remembered. All other religions give you conscience. Zen gives you consciousness. Conscience means, "This is good, that is bad. Do this, don't do that." Consciousness simply means, "Be a mirror—reflect, respond." Response is right, reaction is wrong. To be responsible does not mean to follow certain rules; to be responsible means to be capable of response.

Zen makes you luminous from within. Not an imposition from the outside, not cultivation from the outside; it does not give you an armor, a defense mechanism. It does not bother about your periphery, it simply creates a lamp inside at your center, at your very center. And that light goes on growing . . . and one day your whole personality is luminous.

How did this Zen attitude, this approach, arise? It arose out of meditation. It is the ultimate peak of a meditative consciousness. If you meditate, by and by you will see—everything is good, everything is as it should be. *Tathata*, suchness, arises. Then, seeing a thief you don't think that he should be transformed—you simply respond. Then you don't think that he is bad. And when you don't think about a man that he is bad, evil, you are creating a possibility for the man to be transformed. You are accepting the man as he is. And through that acceptance is transformation.

Have you watched it happen in your life too? Whenever somebody accepts you utterly, unconditionally, you start changing. His acceptance gives you such courage . . . . When there is somebody who simply loves you as you are, have you not seen the miracle happening that something changes, immediately starts changing, fast? The very acceptance that you are loved as you are—nothing is expected of you—gives you soul, makes you integrated, makes you confident, gives you trust. Makes you feel that you *are*. That you need not fulfill expectations, that you can BE, that your original being is respected.

Even if you can find a single person who respects you utterly—because all judgment is disrespect—who accepts you as you are, who does not make any demand on you, who says, "Be as you are. Be authentically yourself. I love you. I love you, not what you do. I love you as you are in your self, your innermost core; I am not worried about your periphery and your clothes. I love your being—not what you have. I am not concerned with what you have, I am concerned only with one thing—what you are. And you are tremendously beautiful" . . .

That's what love is. That's why love is such nourishment. When you can find a woman or a man who simply loves you—for no reason at all, just for love's sake—love transforms. Suddenly you are another person, one you have never been. Suddenly all sadness has disappeared, all dullness is gone. Suddenly you find a dance in your step, a song in your heart. You start moving in a different way—a grace arises.

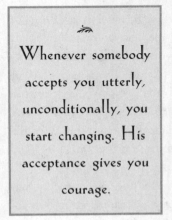

Whenever somebody accepts you utterly, unconditionally, you start changing. His acceptance gives you courage.

Watch it: whenever somebody loves you, the very phenomenon of love is enough. Your coldness disappears, you start warming up. Your heart is no longer indifferent towards the world. You look at flowers more, you look at the sky more—the sky has a message . . . because a woman has looked into your eyes, or a man has looked into your eyes and has accepted you utterly, with no expectation. But this does not last, because people are so foolish. This honeymoon, sooner or later, disappears—a week, two weeks, three weeks at the most. Sooner or later the woman starts expecting and the man starts expecting, "Do this. Don't do that." And again you are pulled back, you are no longer in the sky. Again you are burdened, love has disappeared. Now the woman is more interested in your purse. Now the man is more interested in his food. Arranging the family, arranging the house, and a thousand and one details—but you are no longer in tune with each other's being.

If that harmony remains, then everything is okay. You can go on doing a thousand and one things, nothing is disturbed. But if that harmony is lost; you start taking each other for granted. Within those three weeks you have labeled each other. The day your labeling is complete, the honeymoon is over.

Zen believes in love. It does not believe in rules, regulations. It does not believe in any outer discipline, it believes in the inner. It comes out of love, it comes out of respect, out of trust. When you meditate, you start trusting existence. See the difference: if you ask a Christian or a Hindu, trust is the first demand. He says, "Trust existence—then you will know what God is." In Zen, that is not the first demand. Zen says: Meditate. Out of meditation trust arises, and trust makes existence divine. *Tathata* arises, suchness arises.

How can you go on condemning if you know everything is godly? The so-called Vedantins in India say "All is Brahma"—but still they go on condemning. Still they go on saying that one is a sinner and one is a saint, and the saint will go to heaven and the sinner will go to hell. This seems absurd, if all is Brahma, all is God. Then how can you be a sinner? Then it is God who is a sinner in you. How can God go to hell?

Zen says the day you know all is divine, everything is God. But they don't use the word "god" at all—because the other religions have corrupted the word so badly, contaminated it, polluted it, poisoned it. They don't use the word "god." When you meditate, and by and by you start seeing things as they are, and you start trusting and respecting things as they are, a trust arises. That trust is *tataata*—suchness.

Tathata leads to a vision of the interrelatedness of existence. Then the whole universe is one unit, functioning in an organic unity. They have a particular word for it, they call it *"jiji muge hokkai"*—when you come to know that the whole existence is unitary—it is really a universe, not a multiverse—that everything is joined with everything else; that sinners and saints all alike are part of one net, they are not separate; that good and bad are joined together. Just as dark and light are joined together, just as death and life are joined together, so are good and bad.

Everything is interconnected. It is a web, a beautiful pattern.

Listen to these words of Berenson:

"It was a morning in early summer. A silver haze shimmered and trembled over the lime trees. The air was laden with a caress. I remember . . . that I climbed a tree-stump and felt suddenly immersed in *itness*. I did not call it by that name; in that state of mind there was no word. It was not even a feeling. I had no need for words. It and I were one. Simply it was there, a benediction."

Tathata means coming to a moment when you suddenly see that existence is one, interrelated, dancing in one dance, an orchestra. And all is needed—the bad is as much needed as the good. Jesus alone won't do, Judas is a must. Without Judas, Jesus will not be so rich. Cut Judas out of the Bible and the Bible loses much. Drop Judas out of the Bible and where is Jesus? What is Jesus? Judas gives contrast; he creates the background. He becomes the dark cloud in which Jesus becomes a silver lining. Without the dark cloud there are no silver linings. Jesus must feel thankful to Judas. And it is no accident that when he washed the feet of his disciples, the first feet he washed were those of Judas. Then when he was taking his leave, saying good-bye, he hugged Judas more than anybody else, he kissed Judas more than anybody else. He was his foremost disciple.

Now, this is a mystery behind a mystery. There are rumors in esoteric circles, down the ages, that it was all planned by Jesus himself. Gurdjieff believed that very much. And there is every possibility that Judas was simply following orders from Jesus—to betray him, to go and sell him to the enemies. And that looks more logical. Because however bad the man Judas may have been, just to sell Jesus for thirty pieces of silver? . . . seems too much. Judas had been with Jesus for a long time, and he was the most intelligent disciple of all. He was the only educated one, he was the only one who could be called an intellectual. In fact he was more knowledgeable than Jesus himself. He was the pundit around Jesus.

It seems too much, just for thirty silver coins, selling Jesus. No.

And do you know what happened? When Jesus was crucified, Judas committed suicide—the next day. Christians don't talk about that much, but it has to be talked about. Why did he commit suicide? His work is finished—he should go with the master. A man who can sell his master for thirty silver pieces, can you think of him feeling so guilty that he should commit suicide? Impossible. Why should he bother? No, he had simply followed an order from the master. He could not say no—that was part of his surrender. He had to say yes. No cannot be said to the master. It was planned. There is a reason in it: it is only through the crucifixion that Jesus's message has lived in the world. There would have been no Christianity without the crucifixion. That's why I call Christianity "crossianity." It is not Christianity—because just Christ won't do, the cross was needed for it to happen.

When you see the interrelatedness of things, then Judas also becomes part of the game that Jesus is. Then the bad is part of the good. Then the Devil is nobody but an angel of God—and I don't call him a fallen angel. Maybe on a great mission in the world, sent from God himself—maybe his closest disciple.

The word "devil" comes from the same root as "divine." That is indicative. Yes, the Devil is also divine.

Sasaki relates:

When my teacher was speaking to me about *this*, he said, "Now think about yourself. You think you are a separate being, an island. But you are not. Without your father and mother you would not be. Without their fathers and mothers they would not have been and you would not be."

And so on, so forth—you can go to the very beginningless beginning. You can go on moving backwards, and you will find everything that has happened in existence up to now, had to happen for you to happen. Otherwise you would not happen. You are so inter-connected. You are just a small part of a long infinite chain. All that is, is involved in you, all that has passed is involved in you. You are the apex, at this moment, of all that has preceded you. In you the whole past exists. But this is not all. From you will come your children, and their children's children . . . and so on, so forth.

From your actions will come the resulting actions, and from the resulting actions other results, and from other results other actions.

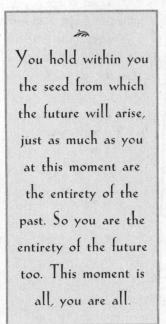

You hold within you the seed from which the future will arise, just as much as you at this moment are the entirety of the past. So you are the entirety of the future too. This moment is all, you are all.

You will disappear, but whatsoever you do will continue. It will have re-verberations, down the ages, to the very end.

So the whole past is involved in you, and the whole future too. At this moment the past and future meet in you, ad infinitum, in both the directions. You hold within you the seed from which the future will arise, just as much as you at this moment are the entirety of the past. So you are the entirety of the future too. This moment is all, you are all. Because the whole is involved in you, the whole is at stake in you. The whole crisscrosses you.

They say that when you touch a blade of grass you have touched all the stars. Because everything is involved in everything else, everything is inside everything else.

Zen calls this involvement of the whole into each of its parts "*jiji muge hokkai*." It is illustrated by the concept of a universal net. The net is called "Indra's Net" in India, a great net extending throughout the universe, vertically to represent time, horizontally to represent space. At each point where the threads of the net cross one another is a crystal bead, the symbol of a single existence. Each crystal bead reflects on its surface not only every other bead in the net but every reflection of every other reflection of every other bead upon each individual bead. Countless, endless reflections of one another—this is called *jiji muge hokkai.*

When Gautam Buddha held the single lotus in his hand, he was showing this *jiji muge hokkai.* Mahakashyapa understood it. This was the message—that in this small lotus all is involved: the whole past, the whole future, all dimensions are involved. In this small lotus, everything has flowered, and everything else that will ever flower is contained in this small lotus flower. Mahakashyapa laughed; he understood the message: *jiji muge hokkai.* That's why the flower was given to Mahakashyapa, as a token of transmission beyond words.

Hence the Buddhist compassion for all, and gratitude for all, and respect for all—because everything is involved in each other.

Now this Zen story:

> One evening as Shichiri Kojun was reciting sutras, a thief with a sharp sword entered demanding either his money or his life.
>   Shichiri said to him: "Do not disturb me. You can find the money in that drawer." Then he resumed his recitation.

No condemnation, no judgment. Simple acceptance—as if a breeze has come in, not a thief. Not even a slight change in his eyes—as if a friend has come, not a thief. No change in his attitude. He says, "Do not disturb me. You can find the money in that drawer. Can't you see I am reciting my sutras? At least you should be that respectful, not to disturb a man who is reciting his sutras, for such a foolish thing as money. You go and find it yourself! And don't disturb me."

Now see: he is not against the thief because he has come to steal. He is not against the thief because he is after money, obsessed with money—no, nothing of the sort. A simple acceptance: this is the way he is. And who knows? This is the way he HAS to be. And why should I condemn? Who am I? If he can be kind enough not to disturb me, that is enough, that is more than enough to expect from somebody else. So don't disturb me.

A little while afterwards he stopped and called out: "Don't take it all. I need some to pay taxes with tomorrow."

See the point—so friendly. There is no enmity in it. And because there is no enmity, there is no fear in it. Because there is no condemnation, such deep respect, he can trust that he will leave. When you are giving so wholeheartedly, you can trust—even the worst of men will at least have respect for your respect towards him. He will respect, you can trust, When you trust somebody, when you don't judge and don't condemn, you can trust that he will trust you. He simply said, "Don't take it all. I need some to pay taxes with tomorrow."

The intruder gathered up most of the money and started to leave. "Thank a person when you receive a gift . . ."

Now, see the compassion of the man. He does not call it theft; he says, "Thank a man when you receive a gift." He is transforming; his vision is totally different. He does not want this man to feel guilty; his compassion is tremendous. Otherwise later on he will start feeling guilty. He was bound to feel guilty—stealing from a poor monk, a poor beggar, who had not much in the first place, stealing from a man who was so readily ready to give, I who accepted you so totally—this man will feel guilty, this man will start repenting. He will not be able to sleep back home. He may have to come back in the morning to be forgiven.

No, that will not be good. Zen does not want to create guilt in any way. That's what Zen is all about, a religion without creating any guilt. A religion can be very easily created with guilt, that's what other religions have done. But when you create guilt you have created something far worse than you were going to cure. Zen does not create any guilt, takes every care not to create any guilt in any-body.

Now he says, "Thank a person when you receive a gift. This is a gift! Don't you know even this much? I am *giving* it to you—you are not stealing it from me." What a difference! It is the same thing.

This is what Zen says: Give—rather than it being snatched away. And this is the total vision about life. Before death comes give every-thing so death need not feel guilty. Give your life to death as a gift. This is the Zen renunciation. It is altogether different from Hindu or Catholic renunciation—they give in order to get. Zen gives in order so that no guilt is created anywhere in the world; no guilt is left behind.

The man thanked him and made off. A few days afterwards the fellow was caught and confessed, among others, the offense against Shichiri. When Shichiri was called as a witness he said: "This man is no thief, at least as far as I am concerned. I gave him the money and he thanked me for it."

You see the point? How respectful! What immense respect! What unconditional respect towards a man—towards a thief!

If this Shichiri were a Christian saint, he would have threatened the man to be ready to suffer hell—and hell for eternity. If he were a Hindu saint, he would have preached him a long sermon on no-theft, and he would have made him frightened that he would be thrown into hellfire. He would have painted a very nightmarish pic-ture of hell, and he would have preached the uselessness of money.

Look: The Zen master does not say anything about the uselessness of money. In fact, instead he says, "Leave a little for me; in the morn-ing I will need it." Money has a purpose. One need not be obsessed, this way or that, for or against. Money is utilitarian. You need not be only living for money, and you need not be against money. It is just utilitarian. That's what my attitude towards money is: Money has to be used, it is an instrument.

In the world of religion, money is condemned very much—the religious people are very much afraid of money. That fear is nothing but greed standing on its head. It is the same greed which has now become afraid. If you go to a Hindu saint with money in your hand he will close his eyes, he will not look at the money. So much fear of money? Why should you close the eyes? He will go on saying that money is dirt—but he never closes his eyes when he looks at dirt. This is very illogical. In fact, if money is dirt he should have to keep his eyes closed twenty-four hours, because dirt is everywhere. Money is dirt? Then why be so afraid of dirt? What is the fear?

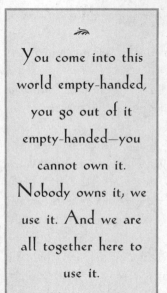

You come into this world empty-handed, you go out of it empty-handed—you cannot own it. Nobody owns it, we use it. And we are all together here to use it.

Zen has a totally different and a very fundamental approach. The master does not say that money is dirt and you should not be looking for other people's money. What does it have to do with people? Money is nobody's. So to say to somebody, "You are a thief," is to believe in private property. Is to believe that somebody can have it rightly and somebody can have it wrongly, somebody has the right to own it and somebody has no right.

Stealing is condemned because of the capitalist mind in the world; it is part of the capitalist mind. The capitalist mind says money belongs to somebody—there is a right owner, and nobody should take it away.

But Zen says nothing belongs to anybody, nobody is the right owner. How can you own this world? You come into this world empty-handed, you go out of it empty-handed—you cannot own it. Nobody owns it; we use it. And we are all together here to use it. That is the message: "Take the money! but leave a little for me too. I am also here to use it, as much as you are here to use it."

Such a practical, such an empirical attitude! And so free of money! And in the court he said, "This man is no thief . . ." He has turned this thief into a friend. He says, ". . . at least as far as I am concerned. I don't know about others—how can I know about others? This much I know: I gave him the money and he thanked me for it. It is finished, accounts are closed. He does not owe it to me anymore. He has thanked me for it—what else can one do?"

At the most we can give thanks. We can thank existence for all that it has given us—what else can we do?

After he had finished his prison term, the man went to Shichiri and became his disciple.

What else can you do with such a man as Shichiri? You have to become a disciple. He has converted a thief into a sannyasin. This is the alchemy of a master, he never misses any opportunity. Whatsoever opportunity is there, he uses it—even if a thief comes to a master, he will return a sannyasin.

To come in contact with a master is to be transformed. You may have come for something else, you may not have come for the master at all—the thief was not there for the master. In fact, had he known that in this hut lives a master, he would not have dared at all. He had come only for the money; he had stumbled upon the master by accident. But even if you meet a buddha by accident, it is going to change you utterly. You will never be the same man again.

Many of you are here just by accident. You were not searching for me, you were not seeking for me. By a thousand and one accidents you have arrived here. But it becomes more and more difficult to go.

A master does not preach, he never says what should be done. Bodhidharma says, "Zen has nothing to say, but Zen has much to show." This master showed a way to this thief. He changed this man, and he changed him with such skill. He must have been a great surgeon—he operated on this man's heart . . . and no sound was heard. He destroyed this man utterly, and he created this man again. And the man was not even aware what had happened. This is what the miracle of a master is.

A Zen sutra says: "The man of understanding does not reject error." When I came across it, my heart danced. Recite this sutra in the deepest core of your heart: The man of understanding does not reject error.

And another master, speaking on the sutra, commented—his name was Ohasama—he commented: "Truth does not need to be sought first, for it is present everywhere, even in error. Hence who rejects error rejects truth."

Tremendous these people are! One who rejects error rejects truth. Do you see the beauty of it? The radical, the revolutionary, standpoint of it? Shichiri did not reject the man because he was a thief; he does not reject the man because of his error—because behind that error is a divine existence, a god. Reject the error, and you reject the god too. Reject the error, and you reject the truth that is hidden behind it.

He accepts the error in order to accept the truth. Once the truth arises, is accepted, spreads, the error will disappear on its own accord. You need not fight with darkness—that is the meaning. Simply light a candle. You need not fight with darkness, just light a candle. The master lighted a candle in the man.

Exactly the same, but a little more Zen, there is another story about another master—almost the same, but still more Zennish.

One midnight when Master Taigan was writing a letter a thief came into his room carrying a big naked sword. Looking at the thief, the master said, "Which do you want—money or my life?"

Now, this is more Zen—he does not give a chance to the thief to say anything. Shichiri at least gave him the chance; with Shichiri the thief asked: *A thief with a sharp sword entered into Shichiri's room demanding either his money or his life.* Taigan has improved upon it. Maybe Taigan followed later on—he must have come across Shichiri's story. He does not give that much opportunity to the thief. He says to this thief, "Which do you want—money or my life? Both are irrelevant—whatsoever you need, you can take. It is your choice."

"I came for money," replied the thief, a little afraid.

This man—he has never come across such a dragon—he says, "What do you want—money or my life?" And so ready to give: "You can choose." No condemnation, nothing of the sort. Even if he had chosen his life, Taigan would have given it. All that has to be taken anyway, it is better to give it. One day or other even life will disappear—so why worry about it? Death is coming; let this thief enjoy a moment.

> *"I came for money," replied the thief, a little afraid.*
>
> *The master took out his purse and handed it to the man, saying, "Here it is!" He then returned to writing his letter as if nothing had happened.*
>
> *The thief began to feel ill at ease and left the room, overawed. "Hey! Wait a minute!" called the master. The thief stood back, shuddering. "Why don't you shut the door?" said the master.*
>
> *Days later, the thief was captured by the police and said, "I have been robbing for years, but I have never been so terrified as when that Buddhist master called after me, 'Hey! Wait a minute!' I am still shuddering. That man is very dangerous, and I have never been able to forget him. And the day I am released from prison, I am going to that man. I never came across such a man—such quality! I held a naked sword in my hand, but that was nothing. He is a naked sword."*

Just these words— *"Hey! Wait a minute!"*—and the thief said, *"I am still shuddering."*

When you come close to a master, he is going to kill you. How can you kill a master? Even if you have a naked sword, you cannot kill a master; the master is going to kill you. And he kills in such subtle ways that you never become aware that you have been killed. You become aware only when you are reborn. Suddenly one day you are no longer the same. Suddenly one day the old you is gone. Suddenly one day everything is fresh and new—birds are singing, and new leaves are growing in you. The stagnant river is flowing again, you are moving towards the ocean.

Another story:

A Zen master had been put into jail several times.

. . . Now a step further! These Zen people are really eccentric people, mad people—but they do beautiful things. "A Zen master had been put into jail several times." Now, it is one thing to forgive a thief, it is one thing not to think that he is bad, it is another thing to go to jail oneself. And not once, many times—for stealing small things from his neighbors. And the neighbors knew, and they were puzzled: Why does this man steal?—and such small things. But the moment he would be out of prison he would steal again, and he would go back. Even the judges were worried. But they had to send him to jail, because he would confess. He would never say, "I have not stolen."

Finally the neighbors gathered together, and they said, "Sir, don't steal anymore. You are getting old, and we are ready to provide you with all that you need—all your necessities, whatsoever it is. You stop this! We are very worried, and we are very sad. Why do you go on doing this?"

And the old man laughed. And he said:

"I steal in order to get in with the prisoners, and bring them the inner message. Who will help them? Outside, for you prisoners, there are many masters. But inside the jail there is no master. Who will help them, you tell me? This is my way to get in and help those people. So when my punishment is over and I am thrown out, I have to steal something and go back again. I am going to continue this. And I have found there in jail such beautiful souls, such innocent souls—sometimes far more innocent. . . ."

172

Once it happened, one of my friends became a governor of a state in India, and he allowed me to go into jails all over his state. I went for years, and I was surprised. The people who are in jails are far more innocent than the politicians, than the rich people, than the so-called saints. I know almost all the saints of India. They are more cunning. I have found in the criminals such innocent souls . . . . I can understand this old Zen master's idea—of stealing, of getting caught, and bringing the message to them: "I steal in order to get in with the prisoners, and bring them the inner message."

Zen has no value system. Zen only brings one thing into the world, and that is understanding, awareness. Through awareness comes innocence. And innocence is innocent of good and bad, both. Innocence is simply innocence—it knows no distinction.

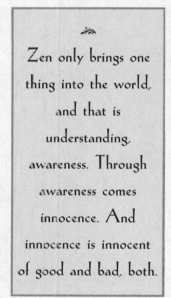

Zen only brings one thing into the world, and that is understanding, awareness. Through awareness comes innocence. And innocence is innocent of good and bad, both.

The last story. It is about Ryokan—he was a great lover of children. As might be expected of such a character as he was, he himself was a child. He was the child Jesus speaks about. He was so innocent that it was almost unbelievable that a man can be so innocent. He had no cunning, no cleverness. He was so innocent that people used to think that he was a little mad.

Ryokan liked to play with children. He played hide-and-seek, he played tamari, handball, too. One evening it was his turn to hide, and he hid himself well under a straw stack in the field. It was growing darker and the children, not being able to locate him, left the field.

Early the following morning, a farmer came and had to remove the straw stack to begin his work. Finding Ryokan there, he exclaimed, "Oh Ryokan-sama! What are you doing here?"

The master answered, "Hush! Don't talk so loud, the children will find me."

The whole night under that straw he is waiting for the children! Such innocence is Zen, and such innocence is divine. Such innocence knows no distinctions between good and bad, knows no distinctions between this world and that, knows no distinction between this and that. Such innocence is what suchness is.

And this suchness is the innermost core of religiousness.

About the Author

∼🪶∼

Osho's teachings defy categorization, covering everything from the individual quest for meaning to the most urgent social and political issues facing society today. His books are not written but are transcribed from audio and video recordings of extemporaneous talks given to international audiences over a period of thirty-five years. Osho has been described by the *Sunday Times* in London as one of the "1000 Makers of the 20th Century" and by American author Tom Robbins as "the most dangerous man since Jesus Christ."

About his own work Osho has said that he is helping to create the conditions for the birth of a new kind of human being. He has often characterized this new human being as "Zorba the Buddha"—capable both of enjoying the earthy pleasures of a Zorba the Greek and the silent serenity of a Gautam Buddha. Running like a thread through all aspects of Osho's work is a vision that encompasses both the timeless wisdom of the East and the highest potential of Western science and technology.

Osho is also known for his revolutionary contribution to the science of inner transformation, with an approach to meditation that acknowledges the accelerated pace of contemporary life. His unique "Active Meditations" are designed to first release the accumulated stresses of body and mind, so that it is easier to experience the thought-free and relaxed state of meditation.

Two autobiographical works by the author are available:

Autobiography of a Spiritually Incorrect Mystic, St. Martin's Press, New York

Glimpses of a Golden Childhood, Rebel Publishing, India

OSHO International Meditation Resort

≈

T he Osho International Meditation Resort is a great place for holidays and a place where people can have a direct personal experience of a new way of living with more alertness, relaxation, and fun. Located about one hundred miles southeast of Mumbai in Pune, India, the resort offers a variety of programs to thousands of people who visit each year from more than one hundred countries around the world. Originally developed as a summer retreat for maharajas and wealthy British colonialists, Pune is now a thriving modern city that is home to a number of universities and high-tech industries. The Meditation Resort spreads over forty acres in a tree-lined suburb known as Koregaon Park. The resort campus provides accommodation for a limited number of guests in a new "Guesthouse," and there is a plentiful variety of nearby hotels and private apartments available for stays of a few days up to several months.

Resort programs are all based in the Osho vision of a qualitatively new kind of human being who is able both to participate creatively in everyday life and to relax into silence and meditation. Most programs take place in modern, air-conditioned facilities and include a variety of individual sessions, courses, and workshops covering everything from creative arts to holistic health treatments, personal transformation and therapy, esoteric sciences, the Zen approach to sports and recreation, relationship issues, and significant life transitions for men and women. Individual sessions and group workshops are offered throughout the year, alongside a full daily schedule of meditations. Outdoor cafes and restaurants within the resort grounds serve both traditional Indian fare and a choice of international dishes, all made with organically grown vegetables from the resort's own farm. The campus has its own private supply of safe, filtered water. www.osho.com/resort.

For more information:

www.osho.com

A comprehensive web site in several languages that includes an online tour of the Meditation Resort and a calendar of its course offerings, a catalogue of books and tapes, a list of Osho information centers worldwide, and selections from Osho's talks.

Osho International
New York
Email: oshointernational@oshointernational.com
www.osho.com/oshointernational

OSHO®

LOOK WITHIN...

BODY MIND BALANCING: USING YOUR MIND TO HEAL YOUR BODY

Developed by Osho, BODY MIND BALANCING is a relaxation and meditation process for reconnecting with your body, complete with a guided audio process. The guided meditation and relaxation process, "Reminding Yourself of the Forgotten Language of Talking to Your BodyMind," accompanies the text on CD.

ISBN: 0-312-33444-3 Paperback $14.95/$21.95 Can.

MEDITATION: THE FIRST AND LAST FREEDOM

A practical guide to integrating meditation into all aspects of daily life, which includes instructions for over 60 meditation techniques, including the revolutionary Osho Active Meditations ™.

ISBN: 0-312-33663-2 Paperback $12.95/$18.95 Can.

YOUR ANSWERS QUESTIONED

A collection of intriguing, humorous, and surprising inquiries that will encourage you to consider the world in different ways, from different angles, and in new directions. You never know: you might just find some new answers—and some new questions.

ISBN: 0-312-32077-9 Hardcover $18.95/$27.95 Can.

TAO: THE PATHLESS PATH

Contemporary interpretations of selected parables from the LIEH TZU reveal how the timeless wisdom of this 2500-year-old Taoist classic contains priceless insights for living today.

ISBN: 1-58063-225-4 Paperback $11.95/$17.95 Can.

YOGA: THE SCIENCE OF THE SOUL

Modern yoga emphasizes physical postures and exercises to increase flexibility and aid in relaxation. But yoga has its roots in the understanding of human consciousness and its potential. Explore this potential with Osho's unique insights into yoga and its relationship to the modern mind.

ISBN: 0-312-30614-8 Paperback $12.95/$18.95 Can.

ZEN: THE PATH OF PARADOX

"Zen is not a philosophy, it is poetry. It does not propose, it simply persuades. It does not argue, it simply sings its own song. It is aesthetic to the very core." In this book, Osho calls Zen "the path of paradox" and unfolds the paradox through delightful Zen anecdotes and riddles.

ISBN: 0-312-32049-3 Paperback $11.95/$17.95 Can.

 TAKE A NEW LOOK   www.OSHO.com

 ST. MARTIN'S GRIFFIN

About the DVD

꧁

The enclosed DVD contains one of the original talks by Osho, and has been chosen to give you a taste of the work of a contemporary mystic. Osho did not write his books, he rather speaks directly to people, creating an atmosphere and experience of meditation and transformation.

The purpose of the OSHO Talks is not to provide information or entertainment—although they can be both informative and entertaining—but rather to provide an opportunity for meditation, to experience the state of relaxed alertness that lies at the core of meditation. With this understanding, it is suggested that a time be set aside for viewing the video without interruption.

Here is what Osho says about listening to his talks:
"How to give people a taste of meditation was my basic reason to speak, so I can go on speaking eternally—it does not matter what I am saying. All that matters is that I give you a few chances to be silent, which you find difficult on your own in the beginning."

"These discourses are the foundations of your meditation."

"I am making you aware of silences without any effort on your part. My speaking is for the first time being used as a strategy to create silence in you."

"I don't speak to teach something; I speak to create something. These are

not lectures; these are simply a device for you to become silent, because if you are told to become silent without making any effort you will find great difficulty."

"I don't have any doctrine; my talking is really a process of dehypnosis. Just listening to me, slowly, slowly you will be free of all the programs that the society has forced you to believe in."

"These questions and answers are really just a game to help you to get rid of words, thoughts. . . . Silence is the question. Silence is the answer. Silence is the ultimate truth. In silence we meet with existence."

"These are not ordinary discourses or talks. I am not interested in any philosophy or any political ideology. I am interested directly in transforming you."